Dog Groomii

A Comprehensive Guide for Pet Owners

Samantha D. Thompson

Table of Contents

First Printed 2023.

ISBN:

DIGITAL VERSION: 978-1-77696-903-6

PHYSICAL VERSION: 978-1-77696-902-9

- A New Zealand Made Product

Get A Free Book At: go.xspurts.com/free-book-offer[4]

5

---

1. https://Xspurts.com

2. https://Xspurts.com

3. https://Xspurts.com

4. https://go.xspurts.com/free-book-offer

5. https://xspurts.com/

DIY Haircuts

As a dog owner, you might have found yourself wondering whether you could save some money and give your furry friend a haircut yourself instead of taking them to a professional groomer. While grooming your dog at home can be a cost-effective option, it is important to consider the risks and potential downsides before diving in. This article will provide some valuable tips and guidelines on DIY haircuts for your dog.

The first thing to keep in mind when considering DIY haircuts for your dog is that not all breeds are created equal. Some breeds, such as poodles and bichons, require frequent haircuts, while others, such as chihuahuas and greyhounds, need very little trimming. Additionally, certain breeds have hair that grows continuously, while others have hair that goes through a shedding cycle. Before attempting to groom your dog, it's important to understand the specific grooming needs of their breed.

Once you have a good understanding of your dog's grooming needs, it's important to invest in the right tools. A good set of clippers, scissors, and combs are essential for a successful at-home haircut. It's important to note that human hair clippers should never be used on dogs, as they are not designed for the thickness and texture of dog hair. There are many different types of dog clippers available, so it's important to do your research and choose the one that is best for your dog's coat type.

Before getting started, it's important to prepare your dog for the grooming session. Make sure your dog is calm and relaxed before beginning the haircut, and make sure to have treats on hand to reward them for good behavior. It can also be helpful to have a second person present to help hold your dog in place and keep them calm during the grooming session.

When starting the grooming process, it's important to work slowly and carefully. Begin by using scissors to trim any long hair, being careful not to cut too close to the skin. Then, use clippers to trim the remaining hair, starting from the neck and working your way down the body. Be sure to work in the direction of hair growth to avoid skin irritation and discomfort for your dog.

One of the most important things to keep in mind when attempting a DIY haircut is to never cut your dog's hair too short. It's better to err on the side of caution and leave the hair a little longer than to risk cutting it too short and causing discomfort or even injury to your dog.

Another important aspect of DIY haircuts is to pay close attention to your dog's behavior during the grooming session. If your dog becomes anxious or agitated, it may be best to stop the grooming session and try again another time. It's important to ensure that your dog feels comfortable and safe during the grooming process.

In addition to the physical aspects of DIY haircuts, it's important to consider the potential risks of attempting to groom your dog at home. If you accidentally cut your dog's skin, it can lead to bleeding and potentially serious infections. Additionally, if you are not experienced in grooming dogs, you may not be able to identify potential health problems such as skin conditions or abnormalities.

Choosing the right clipper

Choosing the right clipper for your dog is an important decision that can have a significant impact on the success of your grooming routine. Clippers are an essential tool for maintaining your dog's coat, whether you are performing a full haircut or just trimming a few areas. With so many options available, it can be overwhelming to choose the right clipper for your dog. This chapter will provide you with the information you need to make an informed decision.

There are two main types of clippers: professional-grade clippers and home-use clippers. Professional-grade clippers are designed for use by professional groomers and are typically more powerful and durable than home-use clippers. They are also more expensive and may be too powerful for the average pet owner. Home-use clippers are designed for occasional use and are more affordable than professional-grade clippers. They are also less powerful and may not be suitable for all types of coats.

When choosing a clipper, it is important to consider the type of coat your dog has. Dogs with thick, heavy coats require more powerful clippers than dogs with thin, fine coats. Clippers are available in a variety of sizes and styles, each designed for a specific type of coat. Some clippers are designed specifically for use on short hair, while others are better suited for long hair. It is important to choose a clipper that is appropriate for your dog's coat to ensure a successful grooming experience.

Another important factor to consider when choosing a clipper is the noise level. Some dogs are sensitive to loud noises and may become anxious or frightened when a clipper is being used. It is important to choose a clipper that is relatively quiet to avoid upsetting your dog during the grooming process. Additionally, some clippers vibrate more than others, which can also be unsettling for some dogs. If you have a nervous or anxious dog, consider choosing a clipper with minimal noise and vibration.

The blade size is also an important factor to consider when choosing a clipper. The blade size determines how close the clipper will cut to the skin. Clippers with smaller blades will cut closer to the skin, while clippers with larger blades will leave more hair on the dog's coat. It is important to choose a blade size that is appropriate for your dog's coat and the length you want to achieve.

One final consideration when choosing a clipper is the quality of the blade. A high-quality blade will cut more smoothly and evenly than a low-quality blade. It is important to choose a clipper with a high-quality blade to ensure a successful grooming experience.

In addition to choosing the right clipper, it is also important to properly maintain the clipper to ensure it operates effectively. Clippers should be cleaned and oiled regularly to prevent rust and ensure a smooth operation. Additionally, the blade should be sharpened periodically to maintain its cutting edge.

Basic dog haircut styles

Grooming is an essential part of a dog's life. Not only does it keep them clean and hygienic, but it also helps to prevent health problems. One aspect of grooming that is often overlooked is haircuts. Haircuts are not just about aesthetics but are important for a dog's comfort and health. A well-groomed dog with a good haircut will not only look good but will also feel good.

When it comes to dog haircuts, there are a variety of styles to choose from. The style you choose will depend on several factors, including the breed of the dog, the dog's age, and the dog's activity level. In this article, we will discuss some of the basic dog haircut styles that you can choose from.

Puppy Cut

The puppy cut is one of the most popular dog haircuts, especially for small dogs. The puppy cut is a short haircut that leaves the dog's hair the same length all over the body. It is a low-maintenance haircut that is easy to maintain and helps to keep the dog cool during the summer months. This style is also great for dogs that have sensitive skin or are prone to matting.

Teddy Bear Cut

The teddy bear cut is another popular dog haircut. This style is a longer version of the puppy cut and leaves the dog's hair at a length of around 1-2 inches. It is called the teddy bear cut because it gives the dog a cute and cuddly appearance, much like a teddy bear. This style is perfect for dogs with curly or wavy hair, as it helps to prevent matting and tangling.

Lion Cut

The lion cut is a more adventurous dog haircut. It is a style that is typically reserved for dogs with long hair, such as Shih Tzus or Pomeranians. The lion cut involves shaving the dog's body and leaving a mane of hair around the dog's head and neck, as well as a tuft of hair on the tail. This style requires a bit more maintenance, but it is great for dogs that are active and need to stay cool during the summer months.

Schnauzer Cut

The schnauzer cut is a popular dog haircut for schnauzers, but it can also be used on other breeds. This style involves shaving the dog's body and leaving longer hair on the dog's legs, eyebrows, and beard. The schnauzer cut gives the dog a distinguished and sophisticated appearance, making it a great style for dogs that participate in dog shows.

Mohawk Cut

The mohawk cut is a trendy and edgy dog haircut that is popular among younger dog owners. This style involves shaving the dog's body and leaving a strip of hair down the center of the dog's back, creating a mohawk-like appearance. The mohawk cut requires regular maintenance, but it is a great way to show off your dog's unique personality.

Choosing the right dog haircut style can be a fun and exciting process. When choosing a style, it is important to consider the breed of the dog, the dog's age, and the dog's activity level. It is also important to choose a style that is easy to maintain and suits your lifestyle.

In addition to choosing a haircut style, it is also important to use the right tools for grooming your dog. A good quality clipper, scissors, and comb are essential for a successful haircut. It is also important to keep your dog calm and relaxed during the grooming process. This can be achieved by using positive reinforcement, such as treats or praise, and taking breaks if necessary.

In conclusion, dog haircuts are an important aspect of dog grooming that should not be overlooked. A well-groomed dog with a good haircut

Tips for a successful home haircut

Grooming your dog at home can be a great way to bond with your pet and save some money on grooming costs. One of the most important grooming tasks for your furry friend is haircuts. However, it can be intimidating to attempt a haircut at home, especially if you have never done it before. With the right tools and techniques, you can give your dog a great haircut without leaving your home. Here are some tips for a successful home haircut:

Invest in the right tools: Before you start cutting your dog's hair, make sure you have the right tools for the job. You will need a pair of sharp scissors, clippers, and comb. Clippers come in different sizes, so choose one that is appropriate for your dog's coat length. You may also want to purchase a set of guide combs to help you achieve a consistent length.

Choose the right location: The location where you choose to give your dog a haircut is important. Find a well-lit area where you and your dog are comfortable. Some people prefer to use a grooming table, but a non-slip mat on a stable surface like a kitchen counter can also work well.

Start slow: If your dog is new to haircuts, start slow and gradually introduce the tools. Allow your dog to sniff and examine the tools before using them. You can also turn them on so your dog can get used to the noise.

Brush and bathe your dog first: Before starting the haircut, brush and bathe your dog to remove any mats or tangles. This will make the haircutting process easier and more comfortable for your dog.

Use caution with scissors: Scissors are sharp and can easily injure your dog if not used correctly. Use caution when trimming around the face, ears, and paws. Always cut away from your dog's skin and use a comb to separate the hair you want to cut.

Take breaks: Haircuts can be stressful for dogs, so take frequent breaks to give your dog a break. Offer treats and praise to help your dog relax.

Don't rush: Haircuts take time, so don't rush the process. Take your time and focus on one area at a time. Remember, it's better to take it slow and get it right than to rush and make a mistake.

Watch for signs of stress: Watch your dog for signs of stress during the haircut. Signs of stress include panting, shaking, and trying to move away. If your dog seems stressed, take a break or stop the haircut altogether.

Know when to seek professional help: Not all dogs are comfortable with home haircuts, and some may require professional grooming. If you are unsure about your ability to give your dog a haircut or if your dog is showing signs of stress or discomfort, it's best to seek professional help.

Dealing with Fleas and Ticks

Fleas and ticks are a common problem for dogs, and they can be difficult to get rid of once they take hold. These parasites can cause a range of health problems, from skin irritation and itching to more serious issues such as anemia and disease transmission. However, with the right grooming techniques, you can help prevent and manage flea and tick infestations on your dog.

Prevention

The best way to deal with fleas and ticks is to prevent them from infesting your dog in the first place. Regular grooming is an essential part of flea and tick prevention. Here are some grooming techniques that can help:

Brushing and Combing: Regular brushing and combing will help to remove any fleas or ticks before they have a chance to latch onto your dog. Use a fine-toothed comb to check your dog's fur for any signs of fleas or ticks, paying particular attention to the ears, under the legs, and around the tail. A flea comb can help to remove any fleas that are found.

Bathing: Regular bathing with a gentle shampoo can help to keep your dog's skin clean and healthy, which can make it less attractive to fleas and ticks. However, it's important not to overdo it, as excessive bathing can dry out your dog's skin and make the problem worse.

Tick Checks: Ticks can be particularly difficult to spot, as they are small and can blend in with your dog's fur. Regular tick checks can help to catch any ticks before they become a problem. Check your dog's body carefully after walks, paying particular attention to areas such as the ears, neck, and between the toes.

Treatment

If your dog does become infested with fleas or ticks, there are several treatments that can be used to get rid of them. Here are some common options:

Flea and Tick Shampoos: Flea and tick shampoos contain insecticides that can kill fleas and ticks on contact. These shampoos should be used in conjunction with other treatments, such as flea combs and environmental control measures.

Spot-on Treatments: Spot-on treatments are a type of insecticide that is applied directly to your dog's skin. They are usually applied to the back of the neck and can provide protection for up to a month.

Oral Medications: Oral medications are available that can kill fleas and ticks. These medications usually come in the form of a pill and can provide protection for several weeks.

Environmental Control

In addition to grooming and treatment, it's also important to control the environment to prevent flea and tick infestations. Here are some tips:

Vacuum Regularly: Fleas can lay eggs in carpets, so vacuuming regularly can help to remove any eggs and larvae before they have a chance to hatch.

Wash Bedding: Wash your dog's bedding regularly to remove any fleas or ticks that may be present.

Treat the Yard: Fleas and ticks can live in your yard, so it's important to treat your yard with insecticides to keep them at bay.

Dealing with fleas and ticks can be a frustrating and time-consuming process, but with the right grooming techniques and treatment options, you can keep your dog healthy and free from these parasites. Regular grooming, tick checks, and environmental control measures can all help to prevent infestations, while treatments such as shampoos, spot-on treatments, and oral medications can be used to get rid of any existing problems. By taking a proactive approach to flea and tick prevention and management, you can keep your dog healthy, happy, and itch-free.

Preventing flea and tick infestations

Fleas and ticks are common external parasites that can infest dogs and cause a variety of health problems. Fortunately, there are several steps dog owners can take to prevent flea and tick infestations and protect their furry friends from these pesky pests.

One of the most important steps in preventing flea and tick infestations is maintaining good hygiene for your dog. This includes regular grooming, such as brushing and bathing, to remove any fleas or ticks that may be present. It is also important to keep your dog's bedding and other areas where they spend time clean and free from debris.

Another key factor in preventing flea and tick infestations is controlling the environment in which your dog lives. This can include regular vacuuming of carpets and upholstery, as well as treating outdoor areas where your dog spends time, such as yards or parks. There are a variety of products available, including sprays and powders, that can be used to treat these areas and help prevent flea and tick infestations.

In addition to good hygiene and environmental control, there are several products available that can help prevent flea and tick infestations. These products include collars, topical treatments, and oral medications. It is important to consult with your veterinarian to determine which products are safe and effective for your particular dog, as well as how often they should be administered.

When it comes to flea and tick prevention, early detection is key. Regularly checking your dog for signs of fleas or ticks, such as bites or skin irritation, can help you catch an infestation early and prevent it from spreading. It is also important to be aware of any changes in your dog's behavior or health, as these can be signs of a more serious flea or tick infestation.

If your dog does become infested with fleas or ticks, it is important to take immediate action to treat the problem. There are a variety of products available, including shampoos, sprays, and medications, that can be used to eliminate fleas and ticks. It is important to follow the instructions carefully and consult with your veterinarian if you have any questions or concerns.

In addition to treating your dog for fleas and ticks, it is also important to treat your home and any other pets that may be affected. Fleas and ticks can quickly spread from one animal to another, so it is important to take a comprehensive approach to treatment and prevention.

Overall, preventing flea and tick infestations requires a multifaceted approach that includes good hygiene, environmental control, and the use of appropriate products. By taking proactive measures to protect your dog from these pesky parasites, you can help keep them healthy and happy for years to come.

Grooming techniques for flea and tick removal

As a dog owner, it is important to be aware of the risks of flea and tick infestations on your furry friend. These pesky parasites not only cause discomfort and skin irritation to your dog but can also transmit diseases. Fortunately, there are grooming techniques that can help prevent flea and tick infestations and remove them if they have already taken hold.

The first step in preventing flea and tick infestations is to regularly groom your dog. Brushing your dog's coat helps to remove dirt, debris, and loose hair that can attract fleas and ticks. It also helps to distribute your dog's natural oils throughout their coat, making it harder for fleas and ticks to attach themselves. Using a flea comb is another great way to remove fleas and ticks from your dog's coat. Flea combs have tightly spaced teeth that trap fleas and ticks when you run the comb through your dog's coat.

It is important to regularly check your dog for fleas and ticks, especially after spending time outdoors in areas where fleas and ticks are known to thrive, such as wooded areas, fields, or parks. Fleas and ticks are most commonly found on your dog's head, neck, and ears, but they can also hide in your dog's armpits, groin, and between their toes.

If you discover fleas or ticks on your dog, there are several grooming techniques you can use to remove them. For fleas, you can use a flea comb to physically remove them from your dog's coat. You can also use a flea shampoo or dip to kill any remaining fleas on your dog's coat. Flea shampoos and dips are formulated with insecticides that kill fleas and other parasites on contact.

Ticks, on the other hand, are more difficult to remove. If you find a tick on your dog, it is important to remove it as soon as possible to reduce the risk of disease transmission. To remove a tick, use a pair of fine-tipped tweezers to grasp the tick's head as close to your dog's skin as possible. Slowly pull the tick straight out, being careful not to crush or twist the tick's body. After removing the tick, clean the bite area with rubbing alcohol or an antiseptic.

Preventing flea and tick infestations also involves keeping your dog's living environment clean. Regularly washing your dog's bedding, toys, and other belongings can help to kill any fleas and ticks that may be hiding in them. Vacuuming your home regularly can also help to remove fleas and their eggs from carpets and furniture.

In addition to grooming techniques, there are also preventative measures you can take to keep fleas and ticks away from your dog. Flea and tick preventative medications, such as spot-on treatments, collars, and oral medications, are available from your veterinarian. These medications work by either repelling fleas and ticks or killing them on contact.

It is important to note that not all flea and tick preventatives are created equal. Some products may be more effective for certain breeds or ages of dogs. It is best to consult with your veterinarian to determine which flea and tick preventative is best for your dog.

In conclusion, preventing and treating flea and tick infestations on your dog involves regular grooming, checking your dog for parasites, and using preventative measures. By incorporating these grooming techniques into your dog's routine, you can help keep them healthy and parasite-free. Remember to always consult with your veterinarian for advice on the best flea and tick preventative for your dog.

Choosing the right flea and tick treatments

Fleas and ticks are common parasites that can infest dogs, causing discomfort, itching, and even transmitting diseases. Preventing and treating flea and tick infestations is essential for the well-being of your furry friend. There are various options available for flea and tick prevention, including topical treatments, collars, and oral medications. Choosing the right flea and tick treatment can be overwhelming, so it's important to understand the different types and their pros and cons.

Topical Treatments

Topical treatments are one of the most popular ways to prevent flea and tick infestations. These treatments usually come in a small vial and are applied to the dog's skin, usually between the shoulder blades. They are designed to kill fleas and ticks on contact and can last up to a month. There are different types of topical treatments available, such as sprays, spot-on treatments, and powders.

Spot-on treatments are the most common type of topical treatment. They are easy to apply and come in a pre-measured dose that is applied to the dog's skin. Spot-on treatments usually provide a month's worth of protection and are effective against fleas, ticks, and other pests.

Sprays are another type of topical treatment that can be used to prevent flea and tick infestations. These sprays are usually applied to the dog's coat and are effective for up to a week.

Powders are a less common type of topical treatment that can be sprinkled onto the dog's coat to kill fleas and ticks. They are usually effective for up to a week and can be reapplied as needed.

Topical treatments are effective at preventing flea and tick infestations, but they can also have some downsides. Some dogs may have an allergic reaction to the treatment, which can cause skin irritation and itching. Additionally, topical treatments can be messy to apply and may leave a residue on the dog's coat.

Collars

Flea and tick collars are another popular option for preventing infestations. These collars are worn around the dog's neck and release a pesticide that kills fleas and ticks. They can be effective for up to eight months and are easy to use.

Collars are a good option for dogs that don't like topical treatments or for owners who don't want to deal with the messiness of applying a topical treatment. However, some dogs may be allergic to the collar material or the pesticide used, and collars can also be bulky and uncomfortable for some dogs.

Oral Medications

Oral medications are a newer type of flea and tick prevention that have become increasingly popular in recent years. These medications come in pill form and are usually given once a month. They work by circulating through the dog's bloodstream and killing fleas and ticks on contact.

Oral medications are a good option for dogs that are difficult to apply topical treatments to or for owners who want a convenient and easy-to-use option. However, some dogs may have adverse reactions to the medication, and they can also be more expensive than other prevention methods.

Choosing the right flea and tick treatment for your dog can be challenging, but there are a few factors to consider when making your decision. First, consider your dog's age and overall health. Some treatments may not be suitable for puppies or older dogs or dogs with underlying health conditions.

You should also consider your lifestyle and the environment your dog lives in. If your dog spends a lot of time outdoors, in wooded areas or areas with high flea and tick populations, you may need a more potent treatment. Likewise, if you have other pets in the household, you'll need to consider the risk of cross-infestation.

Seasonal Grooming Tips

Seasonal changes can have a significant impact on your dog's grooming needs. Different seasons bring different challenges and can affect your dog's skin, coat, and overall health. In This chapter, we will discuss some essential seasonal grooming tips to keep your dog healthy and comfortable throughout the year.

Spring Grooming Tips:

As the snow melts and spring blooms, it's time to prepare your furry friend for the warmer months ahead. Spring cleaning is not just for your house; your dog's coat and skin also need a deep cleanse. It's time to say goodbye to the heavy winter coat and welcome the lighter, thinner summer coat.

Spring is the time to give your dog a thorough grooming session. Use a deshedding tool to remove the dead hair and undercoat that has accumulated during winter. Brush your dog's coat regularly to remove any mats or tangles. Use a gentle shampoo to bathe your dog and remove any dirt or debris that has accumulated on the skin. Make sure to dry your dog's coat thoroughly to prevent any fungal or bacterial infections.

Springtime also brings seasonal allergies, which can cause itchiness, sneezing, and skin irritation in dogs. Keep an eye on your dog's skin and coat, and consult your veterinarian if you notice any signs of allergies.

Summer Grooming Tips:

Summer brings warm weather, outdoor activities, and fun in the sun, but it also brings some unique grooming challenges for your dog. The high temperature and humidity can cause your dog to overheat and become dehydrated. Therefore, it's crucial to keep your dog's coat short and well-groomed during the summer months.

Regular grooming can help prevent skin irritation, rashes, and hot spots caused by the heat and humidity. Brush your dog's coat regularly to remove any tangles or mats that may trap heat and moisture. Trim your dog's hair to a length appropriate for the summer months, but be sure not to shave down to the skin as this can increase the risk of sunburn and skin damage.

It's also essential to protect your dog from fleas and ticks during the summer months. Use a flea and tick preventative recommended by your veterinarian to keep your dog safe from these parasites.

Fall Grooming Tips:

The fall season brings cooler temperatures and falling leaves. As the weather cools down, your dog's coat will begin to thicken and grow, preparing for the colder winter months ahead.

Regular grooming during fall is essential to keep your dog's coat healthy and mat-free. Use a slicker brush to remove any loose hair and mats that may have formed during the summer months. If your dog's coat is particularly thick, consider trimming the hair around the ears, paws, and anus to prevent matting.

As the leaves begin to fall, your dog's coat may pick up debris and dirt. Use a gentle shampoo to bathe your dog and remove any dirt and debris from the skin and coat. Be sure to dry your dog's coat thoroughly to prevent any fungal or bacterial infections.

Winter Grooming Tips:

Winter can be harsh on your dog's skin and coat. The dry, cold air can cause flakiness, dryness, and skin irritation. Therefore, it's essential to pay special attention to your dog's grooming needs during the winter months.

Regular grooming during the winter can help keep your dog's coat healthy and prevent dryness and irritation. Brush your dog's coat regularly to remove any mats or tangles that may trap moisture and cause skin irritation. Use a gentle shampoo to bathe your dog and prevent skin dryness. Consider using a moisturizing conditioner to keep your dog's coat soft and shiny.

Grooming for hot and cold weather

Grooming your dog is an essential part of pet care. But, different weather conditions require different grooming techniques. In hot weather, dogs need extra attention to keep them cool and prevent heatstroke. On the other hand, cold weather calls for measures to keep your dog warm and protect them from frostbite. In this article, we will discuss some grooming tips for hot and cold weather.

Grooming for Hot Weather

Dogs do not regulate their body temperature as efficiently as humans, so they are more vulnerable to overheating. Overheating can lead to heatstroke, which can be life-threatening. Here are some grooming tips to help keep your dog cool during hot weather:

Brush Your Dog's Coat Regularly

Regular brushing can help remove excess fur, tangles, and mats from your dog's coat, which can trap heat and make them feel uncomfortable. Brushing also helps to distribute your dog's natural oils, keeping their coat healthy and shiny. Use a slicker brush or a shedding tool to remove loose fur.

Give Your Dog a Summer Haircut

Trimming your dog's hair during hot weather can help keep them cool. However, be careful not to cut too much hair as dogs rely on their coats to protect them from the sun's harmful UV rays. Also, ensure that you leave at least an inch of hair on your dog's body to protect their skin from sunburn.

Keep Your Dog Hydrated

Dogs need plenty of water to stay cool and hydrated during hot weather. Make sure your dog has access to clean, fresh water at all times, especially when they are outdoors. You can also add ice cubes to their water bowl to keep it cool.

Use Cooling Products

You can use cooling products, such as cooling mats or bandanas, to keep your dog cool during hot weather. Cooling mats work by absorbing your dog's body heat, while cooling bandanas use evaporative cooling to lower your dog's body temperature.

Grooming for Cold Weather

Cold weather can also pose a risk to your dog's health. Dogs can suffer from hypothermia and frostbite when exposed to cold temperatures for extended periods. Here are some grooming tips to help keep your dog warm during cold weather:

Brush Your Dog's Coat Regularly

Regular brushing can help keep your dog's coat healthy and free from tangles, which can cause matting and prevent the coat from insulating the dog's body. Use a slicker brush or a shedding tool to remove loose fur.

Keep Your Dog's Coat Clean and Dry

Dogs with dirty and wet coats lose body heat faster, making them more susceptible to hypothermia. Make sure to dry your dog thoroughly after they get wet, whether from rain or snow. You can also use a towel or a blow dryer on the lowest setting to dry your dog's coat.

Dress Your Dog Appropriately

Dogs with short coats or thin fur may need extra protection during cold weather. You can dress your dog in a coat or a sweater to keep them warm when they are outdoors. Make sure the coat fits properly and covers your dog's chest and belly.

Protect Your Dog's Paws

Your dog's paws are also susceptible to cold weather. Snow and ice can cause frostbite, and road salt can cause irritation and chemical burns. Protect your dog's paws by using booties or paw wax. You can also clean your dog's paws after each walk to remove any salt or chemicals.

Protecting your dog's paws

Protecting your dog's paws is an important aspect of dog grooming that often goes overlooked. The paw pads are vulnerable to a variety of injuries, including burns, cuts, and scrapes. Additionally, the pads can become dry and cracked, which can be uncomfortable for your dog. In this article, we'll explore some tips and techniques for keeping your dog's paws healthy and protected.

First, it's important to understand the anatomy of the paw pads. The pads are made up of tough, fibrous tissue that helps to absorb shock and protect the bones and joints in the feet. They are also covered in a layer of skin that helps to prevent infection and promote healing.

One of the most common causes of paw pad injuries is hot pavement or asphalt. During the summer months, the pavement can become so hot that it can burn your dog's paws. To prevent this, try to walk your dog during the cooler parts of the day, such as early morning or late evening. You can also purchase dog booties to protect your dog's paws from the heat.

In the winter months, snow and ice can be a hazard for your dog's paws. Snow and ice can cause frostbite or cuts on the paw pads. To prevent this, consider purchasing a set of dog booties for your dog to wear during walks in the snow. Additionally, wipe your dog's paws with a warm, damp cloth after coming inside to remove any ice or salt that may be stuck to the pads.

Regular paw pad maintenance can also go a long way in keeping your dog's paws healthy. This includes trimming the hair around the paw pads to prevent matting and debris buildup. Use a pair of scissors or clippers to carefully trim the hair around the paw pads, taking care not to cut the pads themselves.

Another important aspect of paw pad maintenance is moisturizing. Dry, cracked paw pads can be uncomfortable for your dog and can even lead to infections. To prevent this, apply a paw balm or moisturizing cream to your dog's paw pads on a regular basis. Look for a product that contains natural ingredients, such as beeswax or shea butter, which can help to soothe and protect the skin.

Regular nail trimming is also important for paw health. Overgrown nails can cause your dog to walk improperly, which can put strain on the paw pads and lead to injuries. Use a pair of dog nail clippers to trim your dog's nails, taking care not to cut the quick (the pink part of the nail that contains blood vessels). If you're unsure about how to trim your dog's nails, ask your veterinarian or a professional dog groomer for assistance.

In addition to these tips, it's important to keep an eye on your dog's paw pads for any signs of injury or infection. If you notice your dog limping, licking their paws excessively, or if you see any cuts or scrapes on the paw pads, take them to the veterinarian for treatment. With proper care and attention, you can keep your dog's paws healthy and protected all year round.

Adapting grooming routines for different seasons

As a responsible dog owner, it's essential to understand that grooming is not just about maintaining the appearance of your furry friend. It's also a vital part of their overall health and wellbeing. However, grooming needs may vary based on the season. As the weather changes, your dog's grooming needs will also change. So, it's crucial to adapt your grooming routine according to the season.

Here are some tips on how to adapt your grooming routine for different seasons:

Spring

Spring is the season when everything comes back to life. But, with the bloom of flowers and trees comes the onset of allergies, pests, and pollen. So, it's crucial to groom your dog accordingly.

Brushing: Brushing is crucial in the spring season as it helps to remove dead hair, dirt, and dander that may have accumulated during the winter months. Brushing also helps to prevent matting and tangling, which can be painful for your dog.

Bathing: Bathing is essential to keep your dog clean and fresh. However, it's important not to overdo it as excessive bathing can strip the natural oils from your dog's skin, leading to dryness and itching. Use a mild shampoo that's suitable for your dog's skin type.

Tick and flea prevention: Spring is the season when fleas and ticks are most active. So, it's crucial to protect your dog from these pesky parasites. Use flea and tick preventive products that are recommended by your veterinarian.

Summer

Summer is the season when the weather gets warmer, and dogs tend to spend more time outside. However, the hot weather can be harsh on your dog's skin and coat. So, it's essential to take extra care during the summer months.

Coat care: Dogs with long coats may need to be trimmed to prevent overheating. However, be careful not to shave your dog's coat too short as it can increase the risk of sunburn. Apply sunscreen to the exposed areas such as the nose and ears.

Hydration: Make sure your dog has access to fresh water at all times, especially during hot weather. Carry a portable water bowl when going for walks or outings.

Paw care: The hot pavement can burn your dog's paws, so avoid walking your dog during the hottest part of the day. You can also apply paw balm to protect their paws.

Fall

Fall is a beautiful season with cooler temperatures and colorful foliage. However, it's also the season when shedding tends to increase. So, it's essential to adapt your grooming routine accordingly.

Brushing: Regular brushing is essential during the fall season to remove the dead hair and prevent matting. It also helps to distribute the natural oils throughout your dog's coat, keeping it healthy and shiny.

Bathing: Bathing is still essential during the fall season, but it's important not to overdo it. Use a mild shampoo and rinse thoroughly to avoid any residue buildup.

Coat care: Dogs with thick coats may need to be trimmed to prevent matting and tangling. However, be careful not to shave your dog's coat too short as it can make them susceptible to cold weather.

Winter

Winter is the season when the weather gets colder, and dogs tend to spend more time indoors. However, the dry indoor air and harsh weather can be harsh on your dog's skin and coat. So, it's crucial to take extra care during the winter months.

Coat care: Dogs with long coats may need to be trimmed to prevent matting and tangling. However, be careful not to shave your dog's coat too short as it can make them susceptible to cold weather. Use a coat conditioner to prevent dryness and itching.

Grooming for Special Events

Grooming your dog isn't just about keeping them clean and healthy. It can also help them look and feel their best for special events. Whether you're preparing for a dog show or a family photo shoot, proper grooming is an essential part of the process. In This chapter, we'll discuss some tips for grooming your dog for special events.

Start with a Clean Coat

Before you begin any grooming tasks, make sure your dog's coat is clean and free of tangles. Use a gentle shampoo to wash their fur and rinse thoroughly to remove any residue. For dogs with longer hair, you may want to use a conditioner to help detangle and soften the coat. Be sure to dry your dog thoroughly with a towel or a blow dryer on a low setting to prevent any skin irritation.

Brushing

Brushing is an essential step in preparing your dog's coat for special events. It helps remove any loose hair and debris, as well as detangle any knots or mats. The type of brush you use will depend on your dog's coat type. For example, a slicker brush is great for longer-haired breeds, while a bristle brush is better for shorter-haired dogs. Be sure to brush your dog's coat thoroughly, starting at the head and working your way down to the tail.

Trimming

If your dog has long hair, you may need to trim their coat to achieve the desired look. Use scissors or clippers to carefully trim any overgrown hair, making sure to trim evenly and avoid any uneven lines or bald spots. If you're not comfortable trimming your dog's hair yourself, consider taking them to a professional groomer.

Nails

Trimming your dog's nails is also an important part of grooming for special events. Long nails can be unsightly and uncomfortable for your dog, so be sure to trim them to a comfortable length. Use a pair of nail clippers designed for dogs, and be careful not to cut the quick, which can cause bleeding and pain. If you're unsure how to trim your dog's nails, ask your veterinarian or groomer for guidance.

Ears

Cleaning your dog's ears is important for their overall health and appearance. Use a gentle ear cleaner to remove any wax or debris, and be sure to dry the ears thoroughly to prevent any moisture buildup. If your dog has long hair around their ears, you may need to trim it to prevent it from matting or tangling.

Teeth

Finally, don't forget about your dog's teeth! Clean teeth can help improve their breath and overall health. Use a dog-specific toothbrush and toothpaste to brush your dog's teeth, being sure to reach all the way to the back of the mouth. If your dog is resistant to having their teeth brushed, consider using dental chews or other oral care products to help keep their teeth clean and healthy.

Preparing your dog for dog shows

Dog shows are competitions where breeders and owners showcase their dogs' beauty, temperament, and behavior. These shows are not only for the breeders and owners to display their dogs, but also a platform to share knowledge and learn from experts in the field. To ensure that your dog is in top shape and stands out at a dog show, proper grooming and preparation is essential. In This chapter, we will discuss the various steps to prepare your dog for a dog show.

Bath Time

The first step in preparing your dog for a dog show is giving your dog a thorough bath. A clean and well-groomed coat is one of the most essential parts of a successful dog show. It is essential to use high-quality shampoo and conditioner that is suitable for your dog's skin and coat type. The shampoo should be applied gently to the dog's coat and massaged thoroughly to ensure that the shampoo reaches every part of the coat. It is important to rinse the coat thoroughly to avoid any residual shampoo, which could cause skin irritation. Once the coat is clean, it is time to condition it. The conditioner should be applied in the same way as the shampoo and left on for the recommended time, as per the instructions on the bottle. After the conditioner is rinsed off, the coat should be towel-dried, and a blow dryer can be used to dry the coat completely.

Nail Trimming

Nail trimming is an essential grooming aspect of preparing your dog for a dog show. Overgrown nails can not only be unsightly, but can also cause discomfort to your dog while walking. Long nails can also cause an unsteady gait and could result in a deduction in points during the show. It is essential to ensure that the nail is trimmed to a reasonable length without cutting too far into the quick. Clippers or grinders can be used to trim the nails, and it is essential to ensure that the dog is comfortable during the process. If you are unsure about the trimming process, it is recommended to take the help of a professional groomer or a veterinarian.

Coat Care

A well-groomed coat is one of the most important aspects of a successful dog show. It is essential to brush and comb the coat thoroughly to remove any mats or tangles. The type of brush and comb used should be chosen based on your dog's coat type. Dogs with long hair require a slicker brush to remove tangles, while those with shorter hair can be groomed with a bristle brush. The coat should be brushed and combed out in layers to ensure that every part of the coat is groomed evenly. It is essential to ensure that there are no loose hairs, and the coat is evenly trimmed. A professional groomer can be consulted if you are unsure about the grooming process.

Teeth and Gum Care

A clean and healthy mouth is essential for your dog to stand out at a dog show. A proper dental care routine should be followed at home to ensure that the dog's teeth and gums are healthy. The teeth should be brushed regularly with a toothbrush and toothpaste that is specifically designed for dogs. The toothpaste should be flavored to make it more palatable for the dog. The dog's gums should also be checked for any signs of inflammation or infection. If any issues are noticed, a veterinarian should be consulted immediately.

Ear Care

Ear care is an often-overlooked aspect of dog grooming, but it is crucial to keep your dog's ears clean and healthy. Ear infections can be common in dogs, and it is essential to take preventative measures to avoid them. A gentle ear cleaning solution can be used to clean the dog's ears, and it is important to ensure that the ear canal is not damaged during the cleaning process.

Grooming for holidays and celebrations

Grooming your dog is an essential aspect of pet care, and it becomes even more important during holidays and celebrations. Whether you're preparing for a family gathering or simply want your furry friend to look their best, grooming is an integral part of the process. In This chapter, we'll discuss some essential tips and techniques for grooming your dog for holidays and celebrations.

Start early

When it comes to grooming your dog for a special event or celebration, it's always a good idea to start early. If you leave it until the last minute, you might not have enough time to get everything done. You should start grooming your dog at least a week before the event to ensure that everything is in order. This way, you'll have time to make any adjustments or corrections before the big day.

Bath time

Giving your dog a bath is the first step in preparing for any event. A clean and fresh-smelling dog is always a joy to be around. However, you should not bathe your dog too often as it may strip away natural oils in their skin. A bath every 2-3 months is enough for most dogs, while some dogs may need a bath more often, depending on their activity level and breed.

When bathing your dog, you should use a mild shampoo that's specifically designed for dogs. You should also avoid getting water in their ears, as it can lead to ear infections. After the bath, use a towel to dry your dog thoroughly, and if necessary, use a hairdryer on a low setting to dry their fur.

Brushing

Brushing is essential for keeping your dog's coat clean, shiny, and tangle-free. Regular brushing can also help to distribute natural oils throughout your dog's fur, which can keep their skin healthy and moisturized. How often you need to brush your dog depends on their breed and coat type.

If your dog has long hair, you should brush them daily to prevent tangles and mats. Short-haired dogs, on the other hand, may only need to be brushed once or twice a week. When brushing your dog, you should use a brush that's appropriate for their coat type. For example, a slicker brush is great for removing tangles and mats, while a bristle brush is good for distributing oils and removing loose fur.

Nail trimming

Trimming your dog's nails is essential for their health and comfort, but it can be a bit tricky. If you're not comfortable doing it yourself, you should take your dog to a professional groomer. However, if you're up for the task, there are some things you can do to make the process easier.

Before you start, make sure you have a sharp pair of nail clippers designed for dogs. You should also have some styptic powder on hand in case you accidentally cut the quick. To trim your dog's nails, start by holding their paw and gently pressing on the pad to expose the nail. Then, use the clippers to cut the nail just below the quick, which is the pink part of the nail that contains blood vessels and nerves.

Teeth cleaning

Your dog's dental health is just as important as their physical health, and regular teeth cleaning can help prevent dental problems such as tartar buildup and gum disease. You should brush your dog's teeth at least once a week, using a toothbrush and toothpaste designed specifically for dogs. Avoid using human toothpaste, as it can be harmful to dogs.

To brush your dog's teeth, start by getting them used to the taste of the toothpaste. You can do this by letting them lick a small amount off your finger. Once they're comfortable with the taste, you can start brushing their teeth. Hold the toothbrush at a 45-degree angle to your dog's teeth and use gentle circular motions to brush their teeth and gums. Be sure to focus on the back teeth, as these are the most prone to plaque buildup.

It's important to use a toothbrush and toothpaste specifically designed for dogs, as human toothpaste can be harmful to them. You can find these at most pet supply stores.

If your dog is resistant to having their teeth brushed, try incorporating it into their daily routine gradually. Start by brushing for just a few seconds each day, and gradually work up to a full brushing session. You can also try using dental chews or toys to help keep their teeth clean.

Regular dental care is important for your dog's overall health and can help prevent dental problems and costly vet bills down the road. So, with a little patience and effort, you can help keep your furry friend's teeth healthy and strong.

Grooming for photoshoots

Grooming for photoshoots has become increasingly popular among pet owners. Whether it's for a professional photoshoot or just for fun, grooming your dog for a photoshoot can help you capture some amazing memories. However, grooming for photoshoots is not the same as regular grooming. It requires some extra effort and attention to detail to make sure your dog looks their best in front of the camera. In This chapter, we'll discuss some tips and techniques for grooming your dog for a photoshoot.

Start with a bath

The first step in grooming your dog for a photoshoot is to give them a bath. A clean coat is essential for a good photoshoot, as it will make your dog's fur look shiny and healthy. Use a gentle, pet-friendly shampoo and conditioner to avoid any allergic reactions or skin irritations. You can also use a coat conditioner or detangler to make brushing easier and prevent tangles.

Brush their fur

After the bath, brush your dog's fur to remove any tangles and mats. Brushing also helps to distribute natural oils throughout the coat, giving it a healthy shine. Depending on the length and texture of your dog's coat, you may need a slicker brush, a pin brush, or a comb. Use a detangler spray if necessary to make brushing easier.

Trim their nails

Trimming your dog's nails is important for a photoshoot, as it makes their paws look neat and tidy. You can use a nail clipper or a nail grinder to trim your dog's nails. Make sure to avoid the quick, which is the pink part of the nail that contains blood vessels and nerves. If you accidentally cut the quick, use styptic powder or cornstarch to stop the bleeding.

Clean their ears

Cleaning your dog's ears is an important part of grooming, especially if you're planning a close-up photoshoot. Use a gentle ear cleaner and cotton balls or pads to remove any dirt or wax. Be gentle and avoid inserting anything deep into the ear canal, as this can damage the eardrum.

Brush their teeth

If you're planning a close-up shot of your dog's face, it's important to make sure their teeth are clean and white. Use a pet-friendly toothbrush and toothpaste to brush your dog's teeth. Start by letting your dog sniff and taste the toothpaste, then gently brush their teeth in a circular motion. Make sure to reward your dog with treats and praise to make the experience positive.

Style their fur

Depending on the type of photoshoot you're planning, you may want to style your dog's fur. This could involve trimming their fur to a certain length, or using styling products to create a specific look. If you're not sure how to style your dog's fur, consult a professional groomer or a pet stylist for advice.

Dress them up

For some photoshoots, you may want to dress your dog up in a cute outfit or accessories. Make sure the outfit is comfortable and doesn't restrict your dog's movement or breathing. Avoid any clothing or accessories that could pose a choking hazard or cause discomfort.

Reward your dog

Grooming and photoshoots can be stressful for some dogs, so it's important to make the experience positive. Reward your dog with treats, praise, and lots of affection throughout the grooming and photoshoot process. Take breaks if your dog seems stressed or overwhelmed, and never force them to do anything they're uncomfortable with.

Handling Grooming Challenges

Dog grooming is an essential aspect of dog care, and it involves different tasks that range from bathing and brushing to nail trimming and ear cleaning. However, grooming can be challenging, and it requires patience, skill, and experience. Some dogs may not tolerate grooming, while others may have underlying health issues that require special attention during grooming. This chapter discusses some of the common grooming challenges and how to handle them.

Matted fur

Matted fur is a common grooming challenge, especially for dogs with long or curly hair. Mats occur when the fur becomes tangled and clumps together, forming knots that are difficult to untangle. Mats can cause discomfort, pain, and skin irritation, and they may also trap moisture and dirt, leading to skin infections.

To handle matted fur, it's important to avoid shaving or cutting the mats with scissors as this may cause injury to the dog's skin. Instead, use a detangler spray or conditioner to soften the mats and make them easier to comb out. Start by using a wide-toothed comb to gently loosen the mats, working from the ends of the hair towards the skin. If the mats are severe, it may be necessary to use a de-matting tool or seek professional grooming services.

Nail trimming

Nail trimming is another grooming challenge that some dog owners find difficult to handle. Long nails can cause discomfort and pain, and they may also break or split, leading to bleeding and infection. However, some dogs may resist nail trimming, making the process stressful and challenging.

To handle nail trimming, it's important to start by getting the dog used to having their paws touched and handled. You can start by gently massaging their paws and rewarding them with treats. Once the dog is comfortable with paw handling, you can introduce the nail trimmer gradually, allowing them to sniff and investigate it. Use a sharp and sturdy nail trimmer to cut the nails, taking care not to cut the quick, which is the blood vessel that runs inside the nail. If the dog resists, it may be necessary to seek professional grooming services or use a nail grinder.

Aggressive behavior

Some dogs may exhibit aggressive behavior during grooming, which can be challenging and dangerous for the owner and the dog. Aggressive behavior can occur due to fear, pain, or anxiety, and it may manifest as growling, biting, or snapping.

To handle aggressive behavior, it's important to start by identifying the underlying cause and addressing it. For instance, if the dog is fearful, it may help to desensitize them to the grooming tools and environment gradually. You can start by introducing the tools one at a time and rewarding the dog for positive behavior. If the aggression is severe, it may be necessary to seek professional training or behavior modification services.

Skin irritation

Skin irritation is a common grooming challenge that can result from using harsh grooming products or techniques. Skin irritation can cause itching, redness, and inflammation, and it may also lead to secondary infections.

To handle skin irritation, it's important to avoid using harsh grooming products or techniques. Use gentle and hypoallergenic shampoos and conditioners, and rinse the dog thoroughly to avoid leaving any residue. Avoid using hot water, as this may dry out the skin and cause further irritation. If the irritation is severe, it may be necessary to seek veterinary attention.

Eye and ear problems

Eye and ear problems are another grooming challenge that requires special attention. Eye problems may include conjunctivitis, discharge, and inflammation, while ear problems may include infections, discharge, and odor.

To handle eye and ear problems, it's important to start by identifying the underlying cause and seeking veterinary attention if necessary. Use a damp cloth or cotton ball to clean the eyes and ears , being gentle to avoid causing any discomfort or injury to your pet. Here are some tips for handling eye and ear problems in dogs:

Eye Problems:

- Signs of eye problems may include redness, discharge, swelling, or squinting.

- If you suspect your dog has an eye problem, it's important to seek veterinary attention right away to prevent further damage or infection.

- In the meantime, you can gently clean around your dog's eyes using a damp cloth or cotton ball. Be sure to use a separate cloth or cotton ball for each eye to avoid spreading any irritation or infection.

- Avoid using any products or medications in or around your dog's eyes unless directed to do so by a veterinarian.

Ear Problems:

- Signs of ear problems may include shaking of the head, scratching at the ears, redness, discharge, or a foul odor.

- If you suspect your dog has an ear problem, it's important to seek veterinary attention to determine the underlying cause and appropriate treatment.

- In the meantime, you can gently clean your dog's ears using a damp cloth or cotton ball. Be sure to only clean the visible part of the ear and avoid inserting anything into the ear canal which could damage the eardrum.

- Avoid using any products or medications in your dog's ears unless directed to do so by a veterinarian.

Remember, prevention is key when it comes to eye and ear problems in dogs. Regular grooming and veterinary checkups can help identify and prevent many common eye and ear problems before they become serious.

Overcoming grooming anxiety

Grooming your dog is an essential part of pet care. Regular grooming not only helps keep your dog looking good, but it also helps maintain their overall health and wellbeing. However, for some dogs, the grooming process can be stressful and cause anxiety. This can lead to difficulties in maintaining good hygiene and health, as well as potentially harmful behaviors like biting or running away. In This chapter, we will discuss how to overcome grooming anxiety in dogs and make the grooming process more enjoyable for both you and your furry friend.

First, it is important to understand why some dogs may be anxious about grooming. Many dogs may have had negative experiences with grooming in the past, such as being clipped too short or accidentally cut with grooming tools. Others may simply feel uncomfortable with the process, especially if they are not used to being touched or handled. Additionally, some dogs may have anxiety or fear related to being in unfamiliar environments or around strangers.

The first step in overcoming grooming anxiety is to create a positive association with grooming. Start by gradually introducing your dog to grooming tools and the grooming process. Begin with short sessions and gradually increase the time as your dog becomes more comfortable. Use treats and positive reinforcement to help your dog associate grooming with something pleasant.

Another way to help your dog feel more comfortable during grooming is to establish a routine. Set a regular schedule for grooming and stick to it. This will help your dog feel more secure and less anxious, as they will know what to expect.

It is also important to choose the right grooming tools and products for your dog. Use tools that are appropriate for your dog's coat type and size, and avoid tools that are too harsh or uncomfortable. Similarly, use grooming products that are gentle and designed for dogs. Harsh or unfamiliar scents can make your dog feel uneasy and anxious.

In addition to establishing a routine and using the right tools and products, it is important to remain calm and patient during grooming. Dogs can pick up on our emotions, so if you are anxious or frustrated, your dog is likely to feel the same way. Take breaks if necessary, and never force your dog to do something they are uncomfortable with.

One way to help reduce grooming anxiety is to provide a calming environment. Play soft music or use a calming spray to help your dog relax. Use a non-slip mat in the tub or on the grooming table to help your dog feel secure.

If your dog is still struggling with grooming anxiety, it may be helpful to work with a professional groomer or behaviorist. A professional can help identify any underlying issues and provide additional training or guidance on how to make the grooming process more enjoyable for your dog.

In some cases, medication may be necessary to help reduce grooming anxiety. Speak to your veterinarian about whether medication may be an option for your dog.

Addressing grooming-related behavioral issues

Grooming is an essential part of a dog's routine care, but it can also pose behavioral challenges for some dogs. Many dogs experience anxiety or fear during grooming, which can manifest in a range of behaviors such as growling, biting, or attempting to escape. In this article, we will explore some common grooming-related behavioral issues and provide tips for addressing them.

One of the most common behavioral issues during grooming is fear and anxiety. Some dogs may have had negative experiences in the past, such as painful grooming sessions, which can lead to a lasting fear of grooming. Additionally, some dogs are simply more anxious or fearful by nature. Signs of fear and anxiety during grooming include trembling, panting, drooling, attempting to escape, and aggressive behavior.

To address grooming-related fear and anxiety, it's important to take a gradual and patient approach. Start by simply introducing grooming tools to the dog in a non-threatening way, such as placing a brush on the ground near the dog and allowing them to sniff and investigate it. Slowly work up to touching the dog with the tool, then moving to more intensive grooming sessions. It may also be helpful to use treats or positive reinforcement to create a positive association with grooming.

Another common grooming-related behavioral issue is aggression. Some dogs may growl or snap during grooming, especially if they are experiencing fear or discomfort. Aggression during grooming can be dangerous for both the dog and the groomer, so it's important to address it promptly.

One effective way to address grooming-related aggression is to work with a professional dog trainer. A trainer can help identify the underlying cause of the aggression and provide strategies for desensitizing the dog to grooming. In some cases, medication may also be helpful in reducing anxiety and aggression during grooming sessions.

In addition to fear, anxiety, and aggression, some dogs may also experience discomfort or pain during grooming. This can be due to a variety of factors, such as matted fur or underlying skin conditions. Dogs may exhibit signs of discomfort or pain during grooming, such as whimpering, yelping, or attempting to pull away.

To address discomfort during grooming, it's important to ensure that the dog's coat is well-maintained and free of mats and tangles. Regular brushing and trimming can help prevent painful mats from forming. If the dog is exhibiting signs of discomfort or pain during grooming, it may be helpful to take them to a veterinarian to rule out any underlying health conditions.

Finally, some dogs may simply dislike grooming and refuse to cooperate. This can make grooming a frustrating and challenging task for both the dog and the groomer. To address this issue, it's important to approach grooming with patience and consistency. Start with short grooming sessions and gradually work up to longer sessions as the dog becomes more comfortable. Additionally, positive reinforcement can be effective in encouraging the dog to cooperate during grooming.

Dealing with sensitive areas

Dealing with sensitive areas during dog grooming can be a challenging task for pet owners. Sensitive areas include the eyes, ears, mouth, and genitals, where dogs may feel uncomfortable or even distressed during grooming. However, proper handling and techniques can make grooming these areas less stressful and more comfortable for dogs. In This chapter, we will discuss the importance of dealing with sensitive areas during dog grooming and tips on how to handle these areas with care.

Grooming sensitive areas is essential for maintaining the overall health and hygiene of dogs. Neglecting these areas can lead to a buildup of dirt, debris, and bacteria, which can cause infections, irritation, and other health issues. For example, a dog with a dirty or infected ear can develop an ear infection, which can be painful and uncomfortable. Similarly, neglected dental hygiene can lead to dental diseases, which can cause pain, bad breath, and even tooth loss.

When grooming sensitive areas, it is crucial to handle dogs with care and patience. It is important to approach the grooming process slowly and calmly, so dogs feel comfortable and safe. Dogs who are anxious or nervous may require a slow introduction to grooming and frequent breaks to help them relax. Here are some tips on how to deal with sensitive areas during dog grooming:

Eyes:

Dogs' eyes are delicate and sensitive, and it is crucial to handle them with care. While grooming around the eyes, it is essential to avoid getting water, soap, or other grooming products in the dog's eyes, which can cause irritation and discomfort. Use a damp cloth or a tear-stain remover to clean around the eyes. If the dog has long hair around the eyes, use scissors or clippers to trim the hair carefully. It is essential to be cautious while handling scissors around the eyes, as any sudden movements can be dangerous.

Ears:

Cleaning dogs' ears is an essential part of grooming, but it can be uncomfortable and even painful for dogs. When cleaning dogs' ears, it is essential to use gentle and safe techniques to prevent any harm or discomfort. Use a cotton ball or a soft cloth to clean the outer part of the ear, avoiding the ear canal. If there is excess hair around the ears, use scissors or clippers to trim the hair carefully. If the dog has an ear infection or any other ear-related issues, it is essential to seek veterinary care.

Mouth:

Dental hygiene is crucial for dogs' overall health and well-being. Brushing dogs' teeth regularly can prevent dental diseases and keep their breath fresh. However, some dogs may feel uncomfortable or distressed while brushing their teeth. Introduce toothbrushing slowly and gradually, and use dog-friendly toothpaste. If the dog is still resistant to toothbrushing, consider using dental chews or toys that can help clean their teeth.

Genitals:

Grooming around the genital area can be uncomfortable and even painful for dogs, especially if they have sensitive skin. Use a gentle touch while grooming around the genitals, and avoid any sudden movements. Use scissors or clippers to trim the hair around the genitals, but be careful not to cut the skin. If the dog has any skin irritations or other issues, it is essential to seek veterinary care.

Skin and Coat Health

Skin and coat health is an important aspect of dog grooming. The coat not only provides insulation but also acts as a barrier against parasites, harmful UV rays, and external irritants. Keeping a dog's coat healthy and shiny is essential for their overall health and well-being. This article will discuss the importance of skin and coat health, common coat issues, and tips for maintaining a healthy coat.

The Importance of Skin and Coat Health

A healthy coat is not only aesthetically pleasing but also plays an important role in protecting a dog's skin from damage and infection. Dogs with healthy coats are less prone to skin issues like dryness, dandruff, and itching. Additionally, a healthy coat is a sign of a healthy dog. A dull coat can indicate underlying health problems such as malnutrition, hormonal imbalances, or parasitic infestations.

Common Coat Issues

Dog's coats come in a variety of textures and lengths, and each breed has its unique coat characteristics. However, some common coat issues that affect most dogs include:

Shedding - Dogs shed their coat as a natural process of replacing old fur with new fur. However, excessive shedding can be a sign of an underlying health issue, such as poor diet or thyroid problems.

Dryness - A dog's skin can become dry due to exposure to harsh environmental conditions, poor nutrition, or underlying medical conditions. Dry skin can cause itching, flaking, and an overall dull coat.

Hot Spots - Hot spots are areas of inflamed skin that can cause intense itching and discomfort for the dog. Hot spots can be caused by a variety of factors, including allergies, poor grooming habits, or underlying medical conditions.

Mats - Mats occur when hair becomes tangled and matted together. Mats can be uncomfortable and can cause skin irritation and infection.

Tips for Maintaining a Healthy Coat

Regular grooming is essential for maintaining a healthy coat. Here are some tips for keeping your dog's coat in top shape:

Brushing - Brushing your dog's coat is essential for removing dirt, debris, and loose fur. Regular brushing can also help prevent mats and tangles.

Bathing - Regular bathing is necessary for keeping your dog's coat clean and free of dirt and grime. However, over-bathing can strip the skin of natural oils and cause dryness and irritation.

Nutrition - A balanced diet is essential for maintaining a healthy coat. A diet that is rich in protein and essential fatty acids can help keep your dog's coat shiny and healthy.

Supplements - Supplements like omega-3 fatty acids can help promote healthy skin and coat.

Regular Vet Visits - Regular veterinary visits are essential for identifying and treating underlying health conditions that can affect a dog's coat and skin.

A healthy coat is a sign of a healthy dog. Maintaining a healthy coat requires regular grooming, a balanced diet, and regular veterinary check-ups. By following these tips, you can help keep your dog's coat healthy, shiny, and free from common coat issues. Remember, a healthy coat not only looks good but also plays a critical role in your dog's overall health and well-being.

Identifying skin and coat issues

Dogs rely on their skin and coat to regulate their body temperature, protect them from external factors, and signal their health and well-being. As such, maintaining their skin and coat health is crucial, not only for their appearance but also for their overall health. Skin and coat issues are common in dogs and can be caused by various factors such as allergies, infections, parasites, and genetics. Therefore, it is essential to be able to identify these issues early on and take appropriate measures to address them.

The first step in identifying skin and coat issues is to observe your dog's behavior and physical appearance. Changes in your dog's skin and coat may be a sign of an underlying health problem. Some common signs of skin and coat issues in dogs include hair loss, bald patches, dry or flaky skin, itching, redness, bumps or lumps, and foul odor. You may also notice excessive scratching, licking, or chewing of certain areas of the body. If you notice any of these signs, it is important to take your dog to the vet for a proper diagnosis and treatment.

One common skin issue in dogs is dry skin. Dry skin can be caused by various factors such as a lack of moisture, poor nutrition, allergies, and skin infections. Symptoms of dry skin include flakiness, itching, and redness. To address this issue, it is recommended to use a moisturizing shampoo and conditioner specifically designed for dogs. You may also consider adding supplements to your dog's diet such as fish oil, which can help improve their skin and coat health.

Another skin issue that dogs can experience is hot spots. Hot spots are red, moist, and itchy patches of skin that are usually caused by bacterial infections or allergic reactions. These spots can be painful and uncomfortable for your dog and can lead to further complications if left untreated. To treat hot spots, your vet may recommend antibiotics or topical treatments to control the infection and soothe the affected area. They may also recommend a change in diet or environmental factors that may be triggering the reaction.

Coat issues in dogs can also arise from various factors such as genetics, diet, and grooming habits. One common coat issue in dogs is shedding. While shedding is a natural process for dogs, excessive shedding can be a sign of an underlying issue such as poor nutrition or an underlying medical condition. To address shedding, it is important to maintain a regular grooming routine and to provide your dog with a balanced and nutritious diet. You may also consider adding supplements to their diet such as omega-3 fatty acids, which can help improve coat health and reduce shedding.

In addition to identifying skin and coat issues, it is important to take preventative measures to maintain your dog's skin and coat health. Regular grooming can help prevent skin and coat issues by removing dirt, debris, and excess hair. You should aim to brush your dog's coat regularly, at least once a week, and bathe them as needed. It is also important to use grooming products specifically designed for dogs and to avoid using human products, as they may be too harsh for your dog's skin.

Diet is also an important factor in maintaining skin and coat health. Feeding your dog a balanced and nutritious diet can help improve their skin and coat health, as well as their overall health. Foods rich in omega-3 fatty acids, such as fish, can help improve coat health and reduce shedding. Additionally, foods rich in vitamins and minerals such as vitamins A, E, and Biotin can help improve skin health and promote a shiny coat.

Grooming for skin and coat health

Dogs are one of the most popular pets in the world, and their grooming is a crucial aspect of their overall health and well-being. Proper grooming can keep your dog's skin and coat healthy, preventing infections and other skin problems. In this article, we'll explore some tips for grooming your dog for optimal skin and coat health.

Brushing

Regular brushing is one of the most important things you can do to maintain your dog's skin and coat health. Brushing helps to remove dead hair and skin, distribute oils evenly throughout the coat, and prevent matting and tangling. The type of brush you use will depend on your dog's coat type - for example, a slicker brush is ideal for dogs with long or curly hair, while a bristle brush is better suited for dogs with short hair.

Bathing

Bathing is another important part of your dog's grooming routine. How often you bathe your dog will depend on their coat type, lifestyle, and any skin conditions they may have. In general, dogs with short hair can be bathed every three to four months, while dogs with long hair should be bathed every six to eight weeks. Use a gentle, dog-specific shampoo and rinse thoroughly to avoid any residue that could cause skin irritation.

Nail Trimming

Trimming your dog's nails is not just about appearance - long nails can cause discomfort and pain, as well as affect your dog's gait and posture. It's important to use a sharp, dog-specific nail clipper and avoid cutting the quick - the sensitive pink part of the nail that contains blood vessels and nerves. If you're unsure about how to trim your dog's nails, consult with a professional groomer or veterinarian.

Ear Cleaning

Dogs with floppy ears are prone to ear infections and other ear-related issues, which can be prevented by regular ear cleaning. Use a gentle, dog-specific ear cleaner and a cotton ball or soft cloth to clean the ear flap and the ear canal. Be gentle and avoid inserting anything into the ear canal, which can damage the delicate structures inside.

Coat Supplements

In addition to regular grooming practices, you can support your dog's skin and coat health by adding coat supplements to their diet. Omega-3 and omega-6 fatty acids, biotin, and zinc are some of the most important nutrients for maintaining healthy skin and coat. Consult with your veterinarian to determine the best supplements for your dog's individual needs.

Watch for Signs of Skin Issues

It's important to be vigilant for any signs of skin issues, which can range from dryness and itching to rashes and infections. Some common causes of skin issues in dogs include allergies, parasites, and fungal or bacterial infections. If you notice any changes in your dog's skin or coat, consult with your veterinarian to determine the underlying cause and appropriate treatment.

Professional Grooming

While regular at-home grooming is crucial, professional grooming can also be beneficial for your dog's skin and coat health. Professional groomers have the expertise and tools to identify and treat skin and coat issues, as well as provide specialized services such as de-shedding treatments and breed-specific cuts. Consider scheduling regular appointments with a professional groomer to keep your dog looking and feeling their best.

Dietary and lifestyle factors affecting skin and coat

Dogs are often referred to as "man's best friend," and as such, we want to ensure that they are healthy and happy. Part of keeping a dog healthy involves ensuring that they have a shiny and healthy coat. However, skin and coat health is not just about regular grooming, as a dog's coat is a reflection of its overall health. Several factors, including a dog's diet and lifestyle, can affect skin and coat health.

A dog's diet is an essential factor in maintaining skin and coat health. The right nutrition can help promote healthy skin and a shiny coat. Dogs require a balanced diet that contains the right amount of protein, vitamins, minerals, and essential fatty acids. A diet that is deficient in any of these nutrients can result in dry, dull, and itchy skin, which can lead to infections and other skin problems.

Protein is essential for skin and coat health as it helps build and maintain healthy skin cells, hair, and nails. Therefore, a diet that is low in protein can result in a dull and unhealthy coat. Additionally, essential fatty acids, such as omega-3 and omega-6, are crucial for maintaining healthy skin and coat. These fatty acids can be found in sources like fish, flaxseed, and chicken. Adequate vitamins and minerals, such as vitamin E and zinc, are also important for maintaining healthy skin and coat.

In addition to diet, lifestyle factors can also impact skin and coat health. Dogs that live in harsh climates, are exposed to pollutants, or swim frequently may be at a higher risk of skin problems. Similarly, dogs that are exposed to high levels of stress may also be more prone to skin and coat issues. Stress can cause an increase in cortisol levels, which can lead to skin inflammation and other problems.

Grooming is also an essential aspect of maintaining skin and coat health. Regular grooming can help prevent matting, tangling, and other coat issues. Brushing a dog's coat helps distribute oils throughout the coat, which can help prevent dryness and promote shine. Additionally, bathing a dog regularly can help remove dirt, oil, and debris from the coat, which can help prevent skin irritation and infections.

When grooming a dog, it is important to use the right tools and products. The wrong product can irritate a dog's skin or strip away essential oils, leaving the coat dry and brittle. Therefore, it is essential to use high-quality products that are specifically designed for dogs. Additionally, dogs with skin and coat issues may require specialized grooming products, such as medicated shampoos or conditioners.

Certain breeds of dogs are more prone to skin and coat problems than others. Breeds such as Bulldogs, Basset Hounds, and Shar-Peis are known for their wrinkles, which can trap moisture and lead to skin infections. Breeds with long hair, such as Shih Tzus and Lhasa Apsos, may also be prone to matting and tangling. Therefore, it is essential to tailor grooming routines to the specific needs of each breed.

Alternative Grooming Techniques

Grooming is an essential part of a dog's overall health and well-being. Regular grooming not only ensures that your dog looks and smells great, but it also helps to prevent skin and coat problems, as well as other health issues. While traditional grooming techniques are effective and widely used, some pet owners are exploring alternative grooming techniques for their dogs. In This chapter, we will explore some of these alternative grooming techniques, their benefits, and considerations.

Waterless Shampoo

Waterless shampoo is a type of grooming product that does not require water to use. This type of shampoo is especially useful for dogs that are afraid of water, have mobility issues, or have certain medical conditions that require them to avoid water. Waterless shampoos are available in various forms, including sprays, foams, and wipes. They work by absorbing dirt and oils from the dog's coat, leaving it clean and fresh. Waterless shampoos are also a great way to keep your dog smelling good between traditional baths.

Dry Shampoo

Dry shampoo is another alternative to traditional shampoo that does not require water. It is a powder or spray that is applied to the dog's coat and then brushed out. Dry shampoo is a great option for dogs with sensitive skin that cannot tolerate frequent baths or for dogs that have mobility issues. Dry shampoo also helps to remove excess oils and dirt from the dog's coat, leaving it looking clean and fresh.

Baking Soda

Baking soda is a common household product that can be used as an alternative grooming technique for dogs. It is a natural deodorizer and can help to neutralize odors on the dog's coat. Baking soda can be used in various ways, such as sprinkling it on the dog's coat and brushing it out, or mixing it with water to create a paste that can be applied to the coat. Baking soda is also an effective remedy for itchy skin, as it helps to soothe and calm the skin.

Coconut Oil

Coconut oil is a popular alternative grooming product for dogs. It is a natural moisturizer and can help to soothe dry and itchy skin. Coconut oil can be applied topically to the dog's coat or added to their food. When applied topically, coconut oil should be massaged into the dog's coat and skin and then left on for a few minutes before rinsing it off. When added to the dog's food, coconut oil can help to improve their skin and coat health from the inside out.

Herbal Grooming

Herbal grooming is another alternative grooming technique for dogs. It involves using natural herbs and essential oils to clean and nourish the dog's coat and skin. Some common herbs used in herbal grooming include chamomile, lavender, and calendula. These herbs are known for their soothing and calming properties and can help to relieve itchiness and inflammation on the dog's skin. Herbal grooming products are available in various forms, such as shampoos, conditioners, and sprays.

Massage

Massage is not only a great way to bond with your dog, but it can also be a beneficial alternative grooming technique. Massaging your dog's coat and skin can help to improve blood circulation, which can promote healthier skin and coat growth. Massaging your dog can also help to distribute natural oils throughout their coat, which can help to keep it healthy and shiny. Regular massages can also help to relax your dog and reduce stress and anxiety.

Considerations

Before trying any alternative grooming technique on your dog, it is essential to consult with your veterinarian. Some dogs may have allergies or sensitivities to certain products, and it is important to ensure that any grooming technique you use is safe for your dog. It

Waterless grooming

Waterless grooming is a grooming technique that allows you to clean and groom your dog without using water. This technique has become increasingly popular among dog owners because it is more convenient and efficient than traditional grooming methods. In This chapter, we will explore the benefits of waterless grooming and provide tips on how to effectively use this technique on your furry friend.

Waterless grooming involves using specially formulated sprays, wipes, and shampoos to clean your dog's coat and skin. These products are designed to remove dirt, oil, and other debris from your dog's coat without the need for water. The main benefit of waterless grooming is that it saves time and is less stressful for your dog. Some dogs are afraid of water, and using waterless grooming products can be a great way to groom them without causing them unnecessary stress.

Another benefit of waterless grooming is that it can be done anywhere. If you are traveling with your dog or do not have access to a bathtub or shower, waterless grooming can be a convenient alternative. It is also a great option for dogs who are prone to skin irritations or infections as it allows you to clean their coat without the need for water, which can exacerbate these conditions.

When using waterless grooming products, it is important to choose products that are specifically designed for dogs. Human grooming products can be harmful to dogs as they can contain ingredients that are toxic to them. Look for products that are made with natural and organic ingredients and avoid products that contain alcohol or harsh chemicals. It is also important to read the product instructions carefully to ensure that you are using them correctly and effectively.

To use waterless grooming products effectively, start by brushing your dog's coat to remove any loose hair or debris. Then, spray or apply the product to your dog's coat, being careful to avoid their eyes, nose, and mouth. Use a clean towel or brush to work the product into your dog's coat, removing any dirt or debris. Repeat the process until your dog's coat is clean and shiny.

In addition to waterless grooming products, there are other alternative grooming techniques that can be used to clean and maintain your dog's coat. One of these techniques is dry shampooing, which involves applying a powder or foam to your dog's coat and then brushing it out. Dry shampooing can be a great option for dogs with sensitive skin or allergies as it does not require water.

Another alternative grooming technique is using a grooming glove. These gloves are made with rubber or silicone bristles that can be used to massage and clean your dog's coat. They are a great option for dogs who do not like being brushed as they are gentle and non-invasive.

Natural grooming products

When it comes to dog grooming, there are a wide variety of products available on the market. However, some pet owners prefer to use natural grooming products for their furry friends. Natural grooming products are made with ingredients that are derived from natural sources such as plants, minerals, and even animals. These products are free from harsh chemicals, synthetic fragrances, and dyes that can be harmful to dogs. In This chapter, we will explore the benefits of natural grooming products and provide some tips for choosing the right ones for your dog.

One of the primary benefits of using natural grooming products is that they are gentle on a dog's skin and coat. Traditional grooming products may contain harsh chemicals that can strip the natural oils from a dog's skin and coat, leading to dryness, irritation, and other skin problems. Natural grooming products, on the other hand, are typically made with gentle ingredients that help to nourish and protect a dog's skin and coat. This can help to prevent skin problems and promote a healthy, shiny coat.

Another benefit of using natural grooming products is that they are environmentally friendly. Many traditional grooming products contain chemicals that can be harmful to the environment. These chemicals can pollute waterways, harm wildlife, and contribute to air pollution. Natural grooming products are typically made with environmentally friendly ingredients that are biodegradable and non-toxic, making them a better choice for the planet.

When choosing natural grooming products for your dog, it's important to read the labels carefully. Look for products that are made with high-quality, natural ingredients and avoid products that contain harsh chemicals or synthetic fragrances. Some natural ingredients that are commonly used in dog grooming products include coconut oil, aloe vera, chamomile, lavender, and oatmeal. These ingredients are known for their gentle, soothing properties and can be particularly beneficial for dogs with sensitive skin.

Another thing to consider when choosing natural grooming products is the type of coat your dog has. Some breeds, such as poodles and bichon frises, require more frequent grooming than others. Dogs with long, thick coats may benefit from a natural detangler or conditioner to help prevent mats and tangles. Dogs with short, smooth coats may benefit from a natural shampoo that helps to promote a healthy shine. It's also important to consider your dog's age and any health conditions they may have when choosing grooming products.

In addition to choosing natural grooming products, there are other things you can do to promote a healthy, happy dog. Regular grooming is essential for maintaining a healthy coat and skin. This includes brushing your dog's coat daily to remove loose hair and prevent mats and tangles. It's also important to trim your dog's nails regularly to prevent them from becoming too long and causing discomfort or injury.

Another important aspect of dog grooming is dental care. Many pet owners overlook this aspect of grooming, but it's essential for maintaining your dog's overall health. Regular brushing and dental cleanings can help to prevent dental problems and keep your dog's teeth and gums healthy.

Using grooming gloves and mitts

Grooming is an essential part of taking care of your dog's health and hygiene. Regular grooming sessions help maintain a clean and healthy coat, prevent matting and tangling, and detect any skin issues or parasites. While grooming brushes and combs have been the traditional tools for maintaining a dog's coat, in recent years, grooming gloves and mitts have gained popularity as an alternative or complementary tool. In This chapter, we will discuss the benefits of using grooming gloves and mitts and how they can enhance your dog's grooming experience.

Grooming gloves and mitts are typically made of rubber or silicone and have small bristles or nubs on the surface that provide gentle massaging and cleaning for your dog's coat. They can be used for both wet and dry grooming sessions and are suitable for dogs of all breeds and coat types. Here are some of the benefits of using grooming gloves and mitts for your dog:

Comfortable and gentle: Unlike traditional grooming brushes, grooming gloves and mitts provide a comfortable and gentle experience for your dog. The soft bristles and nubs on the surface mimic the sensation of a massage and can help relax your dog during grooming sessions. This can be especially beneficial for dogs that are anxious or fearful of grooming, as it can help build trust and create a positive association with the grooming process.

Easy to use: Grooming gloves and mitts are easy to use and require minimal effort or technique. Simply put on the glove or slip your hand into the mitt and start grooming your dog. The flexible material allows you to reach all areas of your dog's coat, including sensitive areas like the face and ears.

Versatile: Grooming gloves and mitts can be used for a variety of grooming tasks, including brushing, massaging, and deshedding. They can also be used for wet grooming, such as bathing or applying shampoo, as the material is water-resistant and easy to clean.

Cost-effective: Grooming gloves and mitts are typically more affordable than traditional grooming brushes and can provide the same level of cleaning and massaging for your dog's coat. They are also durable and long-lasting, so you won't need to replace them as frequently as other grooming tools.

When using grooming gloves and mitts, it is important to follow some basic guidelines to ensure a safe and effective grooming experience for your dog:

Choose the right size: Grooming gloves and mitts come in different sizes, so it's important to choose the one that fits your hand comfortably. A glove or mitt that is too loose or tight can be uncomfortable for your dog and may not provide an effective grooming experience.

Use gentle pressure: While grooming gloves and mitts are gentle, it's important to use a light and gentle pressure when grooming your dog's coat. Applying too much pressure can be uncomfortable for your dog and may cause skin irritation or injury.

Avoid sensitive areas: While grooming gloves and mitts can be used for sensitive areas like the face and ears, it's important to use caution and avoid any areas that may be painful or uncomfortable for your dog. If your dog shows signs of discomfort, such as pulling away or whimpering, stop grooming and consult with a veterinarian.

Clean and sanitize regularly: Grooming gloves and mitts can accumulate dirt, hair, and bacteria over time, so it's important to clean and sanitize them regularly. Follow the manufacturer's instructions for cleaning and storing your grooming tool.

Mobile Grooming Services

Mobile grooming services are becoming increasingly popular among dog owners who want the convenience of having their pets groomed in the comfort of their own homes. These services offer a range of grooming options, including bathing, haircuts, nail trimming, and ear cleaning. They are especially useful for owners who have busy schedules or for pets who may be anxious or fearful in a traditional grooming setting. In This chapter, we will explore the advantages of mobile grooming services, the services they offer, and the factors to consider when choosing a mobile grooming service.

One of the primary advantages of mobile grooming services is convenience. Unlike traditional grooming services that require owners to transport their pets to the grooming salon, mobile grooming services come to the owner's home. This saves time and eliminates the stress associated with transporting pets to a new environment. Additionally, owners have the option of being present during the grooming process, which can provide peace of mind and help reduce any anxiety or stress for their pet.

Mobile grooming services typically offer a range of services, including bathing, haircuts, nail trimming, and ear cleaning. In addition to these basic services, some mobile grooming services offer additional services, such as dental care, flea and tick treatments, and de-shedding treatments. Many mobile groomers also offer customized grooming packages tailored to the specific needs of each pet.

When choosing a mobile grooming service, there are several factors to consider. First and foremost, owners should look for a service that is licensed, insured, and bonded. This ensures that the groomer has the necessary training and expertise to provide safe and effective grooming services. Additionally, owners should look for a groomer who uses high-quality grooming products and equipment to ensure the best possible results.

Another important factor to consider is the groomer's experience and reputation. Owners should look for a groomer with experience working with their breed of dog and who has a good reputation in the community. They can also ask for referrals from friends or family members who have used a mobile grooming service in the past.

In terms of cost, mobile grooming services are typically more expensive than traditional grooming services. However, this is often offset by the convenience and personalized attention that comes with mobile grooming. Owners should also consider the value of the time saved by not having to transport their pet to a grooming salon and the reduced stress on their pet.

It's important to note that mobile grooming services may not be suitable for all pets. Pets with certain medical conditions or behavioral issues may require the specialized care and attention of a traditional grooming salon. Owners should consult with their veterinarian or a professional groomer to determine the best grooming options for their pet.

Pros and cons of mobile grooming

Mobile grooming is a popular choice for pet owners who want the convenience of having their dog groomed without leaving their home. Mobile grooming services offer a range of benefits, but there are also some drawbacks to consider before making a decision. In This chapter, we will explore the pros and cons of mobile grooming.

Pros of Mobile Grooming:

Convenience: One of the primary advantages of mobile grooming is the convenience it offers. Pet owners don't have to leave their home, and they don't have to transport their dog to a grooming salon. The mobile groomer comes to their home, and they can schedule an appointment at a time that works best for them.

Less stress: Many dogs are anxious or stressed when taken to a new place. Mobile grooming can help reduce the stress on the dog since they are in a familiar environment.

Personalized service: Mobile groomers often provide one-on-one attention to their clients' pets, which can be beneficial for dogs that are anxious or have special needs. Mobile groomers can tailor their services to meet the specific needs of each dog.

Individual attention: With mobile grooming, the groomer focuses solely on one dog at a time, ensuring that the dog receives individual attention and care throughout the grooming process.

No exposure to other dogs: In a traditional grooming salon, dogs are often exposed to other dogs, which can increase the risk of illness or injury. With mobile grooming, there is no exposure to other dogs, reducing the risk of transmission of diseases.

Cons of Mobile Grooming:

Cost: Mobile grooming services are typically more expensive than traditional grooming services. The added convenience and personalized attention come at a premium cost.

Limited services: Mobile grooming services may offer limited services compared to a traditional grooming salon. Some mobile groomers may not have access to certain equipment, such as a tub or dryer, which could limit the types of services they can offer.

Limited availability: Mobile grooming services may not be available in all areas. Pet owners who live in rural or remote areas may have difficulty finding a mobile groomer in their area.

Limited socialization: Dogs that only receive grooming services from a mobile groomer may miss out on the opportunity to socialize with other dogs in a traditional grooming salon.

Space limitations: Mobile grooming services require a certain amount of space to set up equipment and work on the dog. Pet owners who have limited space may not be able to accommodate a mobile groomer.

Mobile grooming services offer convenience, individual attention, and personalized service for dogs. However, they also come with a higher cost and limited services. Before deciding on a mobile grooming service, pet owners should carefully consider their needs and the needs of their dog. They should also research different mobile grooming services in their area to find a reputable and reliable groomer. Overall, mobile grooming can be a great option for pet owners who want the convenience of a professional groomer without leaving their home.

Choosing a mobile groomer

Grooming is an essential part of caring for your furry friend. A well-groomed dog looks and feels great, and it also contributes to their overall health and wellbeing. While you can groom your dog at home, you may also want to consider the convenience of mobile grooming services. These services bring the grooming salon to your doorstep, saving you time and effort. But before you book a mobile grooming appointment, there are a few things you need to know.

What is Mobile Grooming?

Mobile grooming is a convenient service that brings the grooming salon to your home or office. Instead of taking your dog to a brick-and-mortar grooming salon, a professional groomer comes to your location in a mobile grooming van or trailer. The mobile grooming unit is equipped with all the necessary tools and supplies to groom your dog, including a tub, grooming table, clippers, and shampoos.

Pros of Mobile Grooming

Convenience: Mobile grooming is incredibly convenient for busy pet owners. Instead of taking time out of your day to drive to a grooming salon, you can schedule a mobile grooming appointment at a time that works for you. The groomer comes to your location, so you don't have to worry about leaving your dog at a salon for hours.

Personalized Service: Mobile groomers often offer personalized service, which means your dog gets one-on-one attention. The groomer can focus on your dog's individual needs and provide a customized grooming experience.

Less Stressful: Some dogs get anxious or nervous in unfamiliar environments. Mobile grooming eliminates the need for your dog to be in a new place with unfamiliar sights, smells, and sounds. Instead, your dog is groomed in a familiar environment, reducing their stress and anxiety.

Health and Safety: Mobile grooming can be a safer option for your dog. At a traditional grooming salon, your dog is exposed to other dogs, which can increase the risk of contracting an illness or disease. With mobile grooming, your dog is the only pet in the grooming area, reducing the risk of infection.

Cons of Mobile Grooming

Cost: Mobile grooming services can be more expensive than traditional grooming services. You're paying for the convenience of having the groomer come to your location.

Limited Space: Mobile grooming units are typically smaller than traditional grooming salons, which means there's less room for the groomer to work. This may be an issue if you have a larger dog that requires a lot of space.

Limited Availability: Mobile groomers may not be available in all areas. If you live in a remote location, you may not be able to find a mobile groomer near you.

Equipment Limitations: Mobile grooming units have limited space, which means the groomer may not have access to all the same equipment as a traditional grooming salon. This may be an issue if your dog requires specialized grooming tools or equipment.

Choosing a Mobile Groomer

When choosing a mobile groomer, there are a few important factors to consider:

Experience: Look for a groomer who has experience working with dogs, especially dogs that are similar to yours in breed and size.

Reputation: Read online reviews and ask for references to ensure the groomer has a good reputation.

Training and Certification: Look for a groomer who has received formal training and certification. This ensures that they have the knowledge and skills to provide high-quality grooming services.

Insurance: Make sure the groomer is insured in case of any accidents or injuries that may occur during the grooming process.

Services Offered: Make sure the groomer offers the services you need, whether it's a bath and brush, haircut, or nail care.

Preparing your dog for mobile grooming

Mobile grooming has become increasingly popular in recent years as a convenient option for busy pet owners. Rather than having to take your dog to a salon or groomer, a mobile groomer will come to you, providing a full range of grooming services right at your doorstep. However, to ensure the best experience for both you and your dog, it's important to properly prepare your furry friend for mobile grooming. In this article, we'll go over some essential tips for preparing your dog for a mobile grooming appointment.

Choose a reputable mobile groomer

The first step in preparing your dog for mobile grooming is choosing a reputable groomer. Do your research and read reviews to ensure the groomer has a good track record with happy clients and satisfied dogs. Make sure they have the proper certifications, licenses, and insurance as well. A good mobile groomer will be able to provide references upon request.

Introduce your dog to the groomer

Once you've selected a mobile groomer, it's a good idea to introduce your dog to them before the grooming appointment. This can help your dog become familiar with the groomer and feel more comfortable during the grooming process. You can ask the groomer to come over and meet your dog, or you can arrange a brief introduction during the first grooming appointment.

Get your dog used to being handled

One of the most important things you can do to prepare your dog for mobile grooming is to get them used to being handled. Practice touching your dog's ears, paws, and tail, and use positive reinforcement like treats and praise to encourage good behavior. This will make it easier for the groomer to handle your dog during the grooming process.

Get your dog used to grooming tools

Another way to prepare your dog for mobile grooming is to get them used to grooming tools such as brushes, clippers, and scissors. Introduce these tools gradually and always use positive reinforcement. Start with short grooming sessions and gradually increase the length of time as your dog becomes more comfortable.

Practice basic obedience commands

Basic obedience commands like "sit" and "stay" can be very useful during the grooming process. Practice these commands with your dog to help them stay calm and still during grooming. Use treats and praise to reinforce good behavior.

Create a calm environment

Dogs can sense their owners' stress and anxiety, so it's important to create a calm environment during the grooming process. Turn off the TV or any other loud noises, and try to stay relaxed and calm yourself. This will help your dog feel more at ease and make the grooming process go more smoothly.

Consider sedation

If your dog is particularly anxious or fearful during grooming, you may want to consider sedation. Talk to your veterinarian about options for sedating your dog during the grooming process. However, sedation should only be used as a last resort and should always be administered by a licensed veterinarian.

Preparing your dog for mobile grooming can help ensure a stress-free and enjoyable experience for both you and your furry friend. By choosing a reputable mobile groomer, introducing your dog to the groomer, getting them used to handling and grooming tools, practicing basic obedience commands, creating a calm environment, and considering sedation if necessary, you can help make grooming a positive experience for your dog.

Professional Grooming Services

Professional grooming services offer a wide range of services to keep your furry friend healthy, clean, and happy. From basic grooming services such as baths and haircuts to more specialized treatments like de-shedding and teeth cleaning, professional groomers provide expert care for dogs of all breeds and sizes. In This chapter, we will explore the benefits of professional grooming services and what you can expect from a typical grooming appointment.

One of the most significant benefits of professional grooming services is that they can help keep your dog's coat and skin healthy. Regular grooming appointments can help remove dirt, mats, and tangles, preventing skin irritations and other skin issues. Professional groomers can also offer advice on how to keep your dog's coat healthy between grooming appointments, such as proper brushing techniques and diet recommendations.

Another benefit of professional grooming services is that they can help keep your dog's nails trimmed and healthy. Overgrown nails can cause discomfort and even pain for your furry friend, and it's essential to keep them trimmed regularly. However, cutting your dog's nails can be tricky and even dangerous, especially if your dog is uncooperative or has dark nails that make it challenging to see the quick. A professional groomer can safely and efficiently trim your dog's nails, helping to prevent injury and discomfort.

Professional grooming services can also help keep your dog's ears and teeth clean and healthy. Ear infections are common in dogs, and regular cleaning can help prevent them. Professional groomers can clean your dog's ears safely and effectively, reducing the risk of infection. Additionally, professional grooming services can help keep your dog's teeth clean and healthy. Groomers can provide teeth brushing services, and some even offer teeth cleaning treatments to help prevent tooth decay and gum disease.

During a typical grooming appointment, your dog will receive a bath, haircut, and nail trim. The groomer will start by giving your dog a bath with dog-friendly shampoo and conditioner, which will help remove dirt, oil, and odors from their coat. After the bath, the groomer will towel dry your dog and use a hairdryer to ensure that they are fully dry. Once your dog is dry, the groomer will trim their nails and clean their ears. Finally, the groomer will give your dog a haircut if requested.

It's important to note that every dog is unique and may require different grooming services. For example, a long-haired dog may need more frequent brushing and de-shedding services to prevent matting and tangling. A dog with skin allergies may require a special shampoo or conditioning treatment to soothe their skin. Additionally, some dogs may require more frequent grooming appointments than others, depending on their coat type, activity level, and overall health.

When choosing a professional grooming service, it's essential to do your research and choose a reputable and experienced groomer. Look for groomers with positive reviews and certifications from recognized organizations, such as the National Dog Groomers Association of America. It's also a good idea to ask for referrals from friends or family members who have used grooming services in the past.

When to choose a professional groomer

When it comes to grooming our furry friends, there are times when it's best to leave it to the professionals. While some dog owners prefer to groom their dogs at home, others prefer to take their pets to a professional groomer. But how do you know when it's time to make that call? In This chapter, we will discuss some situations where it's best to choose a professional groomer.

First and foremost, if you're a new dog owner and you're not quite sure how to groom your dog properly, it's best to take your pet to a professional groomer. They have the knowledge and experience to groom your dog safely and effectively, and can provide advice on how to maintain your dog's coat at home.

If you have a breed that requires regular grooming, such as a Poodle or a Bichon Frise, it's also best to take them to a professional groomer. These breeds have thick, curly coats that can become easily matted if not groomed properly. Professional groomers have the tools and expertise to safely remove mats and tangles, and can also provide breed-specific cuts that will keep your dog looking their best.

Another reason to choose a professional groomer is if your dog has any skin or coat issues. Professional groomers are trained to identify and treat skin and coat problems such as hot spots, dermatitis, and allergies. They can also recommend products that will help soothe your dog's skin and prevent further irritation.

If your dog has a difficult or aggressive temperament, it's also best to take them to a professional groomer. Grooming can be a stressful experience for dogs, and if your pet is prone to biting or growling, it can be dangerous for both you and your dog to attempt grooming at home. Professional groomers have experience dealing with difficult dogs and can safely groom your pet without putting anyone at risk.

Finally, if you simply don't have the time or resources to groom your dog at home, a professional groomer is a great option. They can take care of all aspects of grooming, including bathing, trimming, and nail clipping, and can also provide additional services such as ear cleaning and teeth brushing.

Finding the right groomer for your dog

Finding the right groomer for your dog can be a daunting task. With so many options available, it can be challenging to know where to start. In This chapter, we will discuss the factors to consider when choosing a groomer for your dog.

The first factor to consider is the groomer's credentials. A professional groomer should have completed a grooming certification course and have a license to practice. It is essential to verify the groomer's credentials before entrusting your dog to their care.

Next, you should consider the groomer's experience. A groomer who has been in the industry for several years is likely to have more experience and may be better equipped to handle different types of dogs and their grooming needs.

Another important factor to consider is the groomer's reputation. You can check online reviews, ask for recommendations from other dog owners, or even visit the groomer's salon to get an idea of the quality of their services. A reputable groomer will have a good track record of satisfied customers.

The location and cleanliness of the grooming salon are also crucial factors to consider. The salon should be easily accessible and in a safe neighborhood. It should also be clean and well-maintained to ensure the safety and comfort of your dog during the grooming process.

When choosing a groomer, it is essential to inquire about the grooming products they use. The products should be safe and gentle on your dog's skin and coat. If your dog has any allergies or sensitivities, be sure to inform the groomer before the grooming session.

You should also consider the groomer's availability and scheduling. A good groomer will have a flexible schedule and be able to accommodate your dog's grooming needs.

Communication is another important factor to consider. A good groomer should be able to communicate effectively with you about your dog's grooming needs and any concerns they may have during the grooming process. They should also be able to provide recommendations for grooming products and services to maintain your dog's coat and skin health.

Finally, the cost of grooming services should also be considered. While you do not want to compromise on the quality of grooming services, it is important to choose a groomer whose services are affordable and within your budget.

What to expect during a professional grooming session

Dog grooming is an essential part of keeping your furry friend healthy and happy. Regular grooming sessions help maintain their skin and coat health, as well as keep them free of dirt and parasites. While it is possible to groom your dog at home, many owners choose to take their dogs to professional groomers for a variety of reasons. If you have never taken your dog to a professional groomer before, you may be wondering what to expect during the session.

When you first arrive at the grooming salon, the groomer will typically ask you a few questions about your dog, such as their breed, age, and any health issues they may have. They may also ask about your dog's temperament and grooming history. This information will help the groomer determine the best grooming plan for your dog.

The groomer will then assess your dog's coat and skin condition to determine the appropriate grooming tools and techniques to use. They may also check your dog's ears, teeth, and nails to see if any additional services are needed. For example, if your dog has overgrown nails, the groomer may recommend a nail trim.

Once the assessment is complete, the groomer will begin the grooming process. Depending on the services you requested, this may include brushing and combing your dog's coat to remove tangles and mats, trimming the hair around their eyes and ears, and giving them a bath using dog-specific shampoo.

After the bath, your dog will be towel-dried and then blow-dried using a high-velocity dryer. This helps remove excess water from their coat and speeds up the drying process. The groomer may also use a slicker brush or a shedding blade to remove any loose fur.

If your dog requires any additional services, such as a nail trim or ear cleaning, the groomer will perform these tasks as well. They may also offer additional services such as teeth brushing, anal gland expression, or flea and tick treatments.

Once the grooming is complete, the groomer will let you know and bring your dog back to you. They may offer you some tips on how to maintain your dog's coat between grooming sessions, as well as recommend a grooming schedule based on your dog's breed and coat type.

It is important to note that some dogs may be nervous or anxious during the grooming process. Professional groomers are trained to handle these situations and may use techniques such as positive reinforcement or distraction to keep your dog calm and comfortable. If your dog has a history of anxiety or aggression during grooming sessions, it is important to let the groomer know ahead of time so they can take the necessary precautions.

Grooming Safety Tips

Grooming is an essential aspect of owning a dog. Regular grooming ensures that your dog looks and feels their best while also promoting their overall health and well-being. However, grooming can be a risky business, especially if you're not taking the necessary safety precautions. In This chapter, we'll discuss some grooming safety tips to help you keep your dog safe during grooming sessions.

Use the right tools

One of the essential safety tips when grooming your dog is to use the right tools. Using the wrong tools can cause harm to your dog. For example, using scissors that are too big or sharp can accidentally cut your dog's skin. Using the right brush or comb can make brushing easier and safer. Choose tools that are appropriate for your dog's breed and coat type.

Keep sharp objects away from your dog

Sharp objects like scissors, clippers, and razors should be kept away from your dog's reach. It's essential to keep them in a secure location, like a locked cabinet or drawer. When you're using these tools, make sure you're holding them securely, and they're not in a position where your dog can accidentally knock them over.

Be aware of your dog's behavior

Another crucial safety tip when grooming your dog is to be aware of their behavior. If your dog is showing signs of discomfort or pain, stop grooming them immediately. Signs that your dog is uncomfortable include growling, biting, and moving away from you. If you're not sure if your dog is in pain, take them to the vet for a checkup.

Use non-toxic grooming products

When selecting grooming products, make sure you choose non-toxic options. Some products can contain harmful chemicals that can irritate your dog's skin, eyes, and nose. It's essential to read the label and choose products that are specifically designed for dogs. Always avoid using human grooming products, which can be harmful to dogs.

Maintain a comfortable grooming environment

Maintaining a comfortable grooming environment is another important safety tip. Choose a quiet and well-lit location for grooming. The area should be clean, dry, and free from hazards like electrical cords, sharp objects, or slippery surfaces. Make sure you're using a sturdy and secure grooming table or surface.

Keep your dog calm

Keeping your dog calm during grooming is essential for their safety. If your dog is anxious or scared, they're more likely to be injured during grooming. Try to keep your dog relaxed by giving them treats, petting them, or talking to them in a soothing voice. You can also use calming products like pheromone sprays or CBD treats to help your dog relax.

Don't rush the grooming process

Rushing the grooming process can lead to accidents or injuries. Take your time and work slowly, especially when grooming sensitive areas like ears or paws. You can take breaks in between grooming sessions to give your dog a chance to relax and recharge.

Know when to seek professional help

Knowing when to seek professional help is an important safety tip. If you're unsure about how to groom your dog, seek advice from a professional groomer or your vet. Some breeds require specific grooming techniques, and it's essential to get it right to avoid injuring your dog.

Safe handling of grooming tools

As a responsible dog owner, ensuring your furry friend's grooming routine is safe is essential. Grooming your dog regularly not only helps to keep them looking and smelling great, but it also contributes to their overall health and wellbeing. However, it's essential to remember that improper handling of grooming tools can pose significant risks to your dog's health and safety. In This chapter, we'll explore some important tips for safely handling grooming tools.

Choose the right grooming tools

Choosing the right grooming tools for your dog's coat type and size is crucial. It's essential to select tools that are appropriate for your dog's needs to prevent injury or discomfort. For example, using a slicker brush on a dog with a short coat can be painful and cause skin irritation. Similarly, using a clipper that's too large or powerful for your dog's coat can cause cuts and injuries.

Keep the grooming area tidy

Keeping your grooming area tidy can help prevent accidents and injuries. Make sure to remove any clutter or obstacles that could cause you or your dog to trip or fall. Additionally, keeping grooming tools organized and easily accessible can help prevent confusion and ensure you're using the right tool for the task.

Use grooming tools correctly

It's crucial to use grooming tools correctly to avoid causing harm to your dog. When using clippers or scissors, always keep the blade away from your dog's skin to prevent cuts or nicks. When using a brush, be gentle and avoid tugging or pulling on any mats or tangles. Always use grooming tools in the direction of your dog's hair growth.

Pay attention to your dog's body language

Paying attention to your dog's body language during grooming sessions is critical to their safety. If your dog appears anxious or uncomfortable, take a break and reassess the situation. Some dogs may become agitated when certain areas of their body are touched, such as their paws or ears. If your dog is showing signs of distress, it's essential to stop the grooming session and try again later.

Check grooming tools for damage

Before using any grooming tool, it's essential to inspect it for damage. Broken or dull blades can cause injury or discomfort to your dog. If you notice any damage to your grooming tools, it's crucial to replace them before using them again.

Practice safe restraint techniques

Proper restraint techniques are crucial for ensuring your dog's safety during grooming sessions. Depending on your dog's size and behavior, different restraint methods may be necessary. For example, a small dog may be able to sit still on a grooming table with a grooming arm, while a larger dog may require more hands-on restraint. It's important to find a method that works best for you and your dog to prevent injury or escape.

Use caution around sensitive areas

When grooming sensitive areas such as the ears or paws, it's crucial to use caution. These areas are delicate and require gentle handling to prevent injury or discomfort. Take extra care when trimming nails or cleaning ears to avoid causing your dog pain.

Preventing injuries during grooming

Grooming your dog is an important aspect of pet ownership. Not only does it help your dog look and feel better, but it also contributes to their overall health and well-being. However, it is essential to remember that grooming can be dangerous if not done correctly. Injuries during grooming can be prevented with proper knowledge, technique, and tools. In this article, we will discuss some tips and techniques for preventing injuries during grooming.

The first step in preventing injuries during grooming is to make sure that your dog is comfortable with the process. It is best to start grooming your dog when they are young, so they become accustomed to the experience. If your dog is already an adult and has not been groomed before, start by introducing them to the tools gradually. Use positive reinforcement techniques such as treats and praise to make the experience more enjoyable for them.

Another important factor to consider is the type of grooming tools you use. Make sure that the tools you use are appropriate for your dog's breed and coat type. Using the wrong tools can cause injuries, so it is essential to use the right tools for the job. For example, a slicker brush is ideal for long-haired dogs, while a pin brush is better suited for short-haired dogs.

It is also important to maintain your grooming tools properly. Dull blades or dirty tools can cause injuries to your dog's skin. Make sure that your grooming tools are clean and in good condition before each use. If a tool is damaged or worn out, replace it immediately.

When grooming your dog, it is important to pay attention to their body language. If your dog is uncomfortable or in pain, they may show signs of distress such as growling or snapping. If this happens, stop grooming immediately and give your dog a break. You can resume grooming later, once your dog has calmed down.

Trimming your dog's nails is an important part of grooming, but it can be tricky. Cutting the nails too short can cause bleeding and pain. It is essential to use a sharp pair of nail clippers and to trim the nails gradually, taking care not to cut the quick. If you are unsure about how to trim your dog's nails, consult with a professional groomer or your veterinarian.

Bathing your dog is also an important aspect of grooming. However, it is essential to use a shampoo that is specifically designed for dogs. Human shampoos can be too harsh for dogs and can cause skin irritation. When bathing your dog, avoid getting water in their ears, as this can lead to ear infections. Make sure to rinse your dog thoroughly after bathing to remove all traces of shampoo.

Finally, it is important to be prepared for emergencies. Accidents can happen, so it is essential to have a first aid kit on hand. Your first aid kit should include items such as bandages, antiseptic solution, and styptic powder to stop bleeding. If your dog experiences a serious injury during grooming, seek veterinary care immediately.

Monitoring your dog's health during grooming

Grooming your dog is an essential part of their overall health and well-being. However, it's important to remember that grooming can also be a time for you to monitor your dog's health and potentially identify any issues early on. In This chapter, we'll explore some key tips for monitoring your dog's health during grooming.

The first thing to keep in mind is that regular grooming sessions can help you identify any changes in your dog's skin or coat. Take note of any bumps, lumps, or scabs that you may come across. Additionally, pay attention to any changes in your dog's coat texture or appearance, such as dryness, dullness, or excessive shedding. If you notice any significant changes, it's important to consult with your veterinarian.

Another aspect of monitoring your dog's health during grooming is paying attention to their behavior. Does your dog seem more anxious or uncomfortable during grooming than usual? Are they more sensitive to certain areas being touched or handled? These could be signs of pain or discomfort that should be addressed by a veterinarian. Additionally, keep an eye out for any excessive scratching or licking, which could be a sign of skin irritation or allergies.

When grooming your dog, it's also important to pay attention to their ears, eyes, and teeth. Check their ears for any signs of infection, such as redness, swelling, or discharge. If your dog's eyes appear red or irritated, or if they are squinting or rubbing their eyes excessively, they may have an eye infection or injury. Lastly, inspect your dog's teeth and gums for signs of dental issues, such as plaque buildup or gum disease.

One final tip for monitoring your dog's health during grooming is to check their overall body condition. Does your dog appear to be losing weight or muscle mass? Are they experiencing lethargy or a lack of energy? These could be signs of underlying health issues that require attention from a veterinarian.

In addition to these tips, it's important to establish a regular grooming routine with your dog. This not only helps maintain their health and hygiene but also allows you to monitor any changes over time. During grooming sessions, take the time to bond with your dog and make it a positive experience for both of you.

Overall, monitoring your dog's health during grooming is an important aspect of responsible pet ownership. By paying attention to their skin, coat, behavior, ears, eyes, teeth, and overall body condition, you can potentially identify any health issues early on and ensure your dog stays happy and healthy.

Troubleshooting grooming challenges

Grooming is an essential aspect of maintaining a dog's overall health and wellbeing. However, it can also be a challenging task, particularly when dealing with grooming challenges. Some common challenges that dog owners face during grooming include tangled fur, matting, shedding, and skin issues. In This chapter, we will discuss some troubleshooting tips for these challenges.

Tangled Fur

Tangled fur is a common problem, particularly in dogs with long, thick coats. The easiest way to prevent tangling is to brush your dog's fur regularly. However, if your dog's fur is already tangled, you can use a detangling spray or conditioner to make it easier to brush. Start by gently teasing out the tangles with your fingers or a wide-toothed comb. Once you have removed the tangles, use a slicker brush to brush through the fur thoroughly. Be gentle while brushing, as aggressive brushing can cause discomfort to your dog.

Matting

Matting occurs when the fur becomes tangled and compressed, creating dense knots that can be painful and uncomfortable for your dog. To prevent matting, brush your dog's fur regularly, particularly in areas prone to matting, such as the ears, armpits, and legs. If your dog's fur is already matted, do not attempt to remove the mats with scissors, as this can be dangerous. Instead, use a dematting tool or mat splitter, which will gently cut through the mats without damaging the fur. Alternatively, you can take your dog to a professional groomer, who can safely remove the mats using specialized tools and techniques.

Shedding

Shedding is a natural process for dogs, particularly during the spring and fall when they shed their winter and summer coats. However, excessive shedding can be a sign of an underlying health issue, such as poor diet or stress. To reduce shedding, brush your dog's fur regularly using a shedding blade or slicker brush. You can also use a high-quality dog food that contains essential nutrients such as omega-3 fatty acids and biotin, which promote healthy skin and coat. If your dog continues to shed excessively, consult your veterinarian for further evaluation.

Skin Issues

Skin issues, such as dry skin, hot spots, and rashes, are common grooming challenges that can cause discomfort and irritation to your dog. To prevent skin issues, bathe your dog regularly using a mild dog shampoo, as excessive bathing can strip the natural oils from your dog's skin, leading to dryness and irritation. After bathing, use a conditioner or moisturizer to keep your dog's skin hydrated. If your dog has a skin issue, such as a hot spot or rash, consult your veterinarian, who can prescribe medication or recommend a specialized shampoo or treatment.

Resources:

American Kennel Club (AKC) - https://www.akc.org/

PetMD - https://www.petmd.com/

Pet Health Network - https://www.pethealthnetwork.com/

Online resources for grooming tips

Grooming your dog is an essential part of keeping them healthy, happy, and looking good. However, it can be challenging to know where to start, especially if you're a new dog owner. Thankfully, there are plenty of online resources available to help you learn the ins and outs of dog grooming.

One of the best places to start is with breed-specific grooming guides. Different breeds have different grooming requirements, so it's essential to know what your particular dog needs. A quick Google search of "grooming guide for [breed]" should yield plenty of results, including articles, videos, and step-by-step guides. Some breed-specific websites, such as the American Kennel Club's website, also have detailed grooming instructions.

YouTube is another great resource for dog grooming tips. There are countless channels dedicated to dog grooming, ranging from professional groomers to everyday dog owners. These channels can offer valuable insights into grooming techniques, as well as product reviews and recommendations. Some popular channels include "GroomerTV," "My Favorite Groomer," and "Dogumentary TV."

Social media platforms like Instagram and TikTok have also become popular destinations for dog grooming content. Many professional groomers and influencers post photos and videos of their grooming routines and share tips and tricks for dog owners. Hashtags like #doggroomingtips and #doggrooming101 can help you find relevant content on these platforms.

In addition to these general resources, there are also websites and blogs dedicated specifically to dog grooming. Some of these include "The Spruce Pets," "PetMD," and "Dogster." These sites offer a wealth of information on grooming techniques, product recommendations, and common grooming challenges.

It's important to note that while online resources can be helpful, they should never replace the advice of a professional groomer or veterinarian. If you have specific concerns about your dog's grooming needs or are unsure about a particular technique, it's always best to consult a professional.

When using online resources, it's also essential to consider the source. Always make sure that the website or channel you're getting your information from is reputable and trustworthy. Look for sites that cite their sources and provide detailed information on the authors' credentials and experience.

Finally, it's worth noting that there are many online grooming courses and certifications available for those looking to become professional groomers. These courses can provide in-depth instruction on grooming techniques, tools, and safety procedures, and can be a valuable investment for those looking to pursue a career in dog grooming.

Celebrating your dog's grooming success

As a pet owner, grooming your dog can be a rewarding and satisfying experience. It's a chance to bond with your furry friend and keep them healthy and clean. When you've successfully groomed your dog, it's important to celebrate their success and hard work, just as you would with any other accomplishment. Here are some tips for celebrating your dog's grooming success.

Give them treats

Dogs love treats, and giving them a special treat after a successful grooming session is a great way to show your appreciation. You can offer your dog a small, healthy treat, such as a piece of chicken or a carrot. It's important to avoid giving your dog too many treats, as it can lead to weight gain and other health problems.

Play with them

Playing with your dog is another way to celebrate their grooming success. Take them for a walk or play fetch in the backyard. Spending time with your dog is a great way to strengthen your bond and show them how much you care.

Give them extra love and attention

Dogs thrive on love and attention, and giving your furry friend some extra cuddles and praise after a grooming session is a great way to celebrate their success. Pet them, talk to them, and give them lots of love. This will make them feel appreciated and valued.

Take them on a special outing

If your dog loves going on outings, take them on a special adventure after a grooming session. Take them to a new dog park or a pet-friendly beach. This will give them a chance to explore and have fun, and it's a great way to celebrate their grooming success.

Share their success with others

If your dog has had a particularly successful grooming session, share their success with others. Post a photo on social media, or tell your friends and family how proud you are of your furry friend. This will not only make your dog feel special, but it will also give you a chance to connect with others who share your love of dogs.

When celebrating your dog's grooming success, it's important to keep in mind that each dog is unique, and what works for one dog may not work for another. Some dogs may prefer treats, while others may prefer extra playtime. The key is to find what works for your furry friend and celebrate their success in a way that they will appreciate.

In conclusion, celebrating your dog's grooming success is an important part of the grooming process. It's a chance to show your furry friend how much you care and appreciate their hard work. By giving them treats, playing with them, giving them extra love and attention, taking them on special outings, and sharing their success with others, you can make your dog feel valued and loved. So the next time you successfully groom your dog, take the time to celebrate their success and enjoy the special bond that you share.

Have Questions / Comments?

1

This book was designed to cover as much as possible but I know I have probably missed something, or some new amazing discovery that has just come out.

If you notice something missing or have a question that I failed to answer, please get in touch and let me know. If I can, I will email you an answer and also update the book so others can also benefit from it.

Thanks For Being Awesome :)

Submit Your Questions / Comments At:

https://go.xspurts.com/questions

---

1. https://xspurts.com/posts/questions

Get Another Book Free

1

We love writing and have produced a huge number of books.

For being one of our amazing readers, we would love to offer you another book we have created, 100% free.

To claim this limited time special offer, simply go to the site below and enter your name and email address.

You will then receive one of my great books, direct to your email account, 100% free!

https://go.xspurts.com/free-book-offer

---

1. https://xspurts.com/posts/free-book-offer

Also by Samantha D. Thompson

Printed in the USA
CPSIA information can be obtained
at www.ICGtesting.com
LVHW021551151123
764040LV00010B/390